T0355057

# UNDERSTANDING RESIDENTIAL SAFETY AND SECURITY IN CANADA

*A Comprehensive Guide for Property
Managers to keep their Property
and Residents safe*

SCOTT HILL, CPP, RCM, PSP

Order this book online at www.trafford.com
or email orders@trafford.com

Most Trafford titles are also available at major online book retailers.

© Copyright 2025 Scott Hill, CPP, RCM, PSP.
All rights reserved. No part of this publication may be reproduced, stored in a retrieval
system, or transmitted, in any form or by any means, electronic, mechanical, photocopying,
recording, or otherwise, without the written prior permission of the author.

Print information available on the last page.

ISBN: 978-1-6987-1874-3 (sc)
ISBN: 978-1-6987-1873-6 (e)

Library of Congress Control Number: 2025900532

Because of the dynamic nature of the Internet, any web addresses or links contained in
this book may have changed since publication and may no longer be valid. The views
expressed in this work are solely those of the author and do not necessarily reflect the
views of the publisher, and the publisher hereby disclaims any responsibility for them.

Any people depicted in stock imagery provided by Getty Images are models, and such images are
being used for illustrative purposes only.
Certain stock imagery © Getty Images.

*Trafford rev. 01/20/2025*

 www.trafford.com
North America & international
toll-free: 844-688-6899 (USA & Canada)
fax: 812 355 4082

# DEDICATION

**To Mr. Doug Smith,**

A mentor, a guide, and a man amongst men. Your guidance, motivation, friendship, and unwavering dedication to the principles of honour and security have left an indelible mark on me and my progress. Thank you for your support on this amazing journey and for inspiring me to strive for security excellence every step of the way. This book is as much a testament to your influence as it is to the lessons you've imparted.

**To (Mary) Sam,**

My wife, best friend, and greatest supporter.

Thank you for your endless patience in my big dreams, and our love that sustains me through every obstacle, roadblock, dream and ambition.

This book is as much yours as it is mine—for every late night I was gone, every sacrificed moment we missed together, and every moment you stood by me, cheering me on. I am forever grateful – Love you always!

# CONTENTS

About the Author ............................................................. ix

Introduction ..................................................................... xi

Chapter 1    Understanding Residential and Condominium
             Security in Canada ........................................... 1

Chapter 2    Perimeter Protection ......................................... 19

Chapter 3    Access Control ................................................ 28

Chapter 4    Security Lighting ............................................. 49

Chapter 5    Video Surveillance Systems ................................. 61

Chapter 6    Crime Prevention through Environmental Design
             (CPTED) ....................................................... 73

Chapter 7    Security and Concierge Services ........................... 87

Chapter 8    Miscellaneous and Final Thoughts ....................... 110

Appendix: Security Checklist ............................................. 131

Appendix: Lighting Levels ................................................. 143

Appendix: Risk Rating ..................................................... 145

Appendix: Signage (Private Property) ................................... 147

Appendix: Signage (Reduce Tailgating) ................................. 149

# ABOUT THE AUTHOR

## *Scott Hill, RCM, CPP, PSP*

Scott Hill has an extensive background in condominium management and security, with a career span of over three decades. He served as a condominium manager from 2003 to 2017, gaining firsthand experience in the day-to-day operations and security needs of residential properties.

Scott obtained his Registered Condominium Manager (RCM) designation in 2012, enhancing his professional credentials and expertise in managing condominium properties effectively. In 2015, he achieved the Physical Security Professional (PSP) certification, a designation that recognizes his advanced knowledge and skills in threat assessment, integrated physical security systems, and the appropriate application of security measures. Further solidifying his expertise, Scott earned the Certified Professional (CPP) designation in 2022, which is the gold standard for security management professionals worldwide. The CPP certification signifies his mastery in security management, including planning, implementation, and management of security programs.

Throughout his career, Scott has conducted over 50 security audits for condominiums and residential buildings across Ontario, providing valuable insights and recommendations to enhance the safety and security of residential communities. His commitment to improving condominium security is evident in his prolific writing; he has authored fifteen articles on facility security, and they have been published in respected publications such as Canadian Security Magazine, CondoContact, CondoBusiness, CM Magazine, and SP&T News.

As a motivated and enthusiastic speaker, Scott is frequently called upon to share his expertise on building security and emergency management. He has spoken at numerous events for organizations like

ACMO, the Condominium Directors Group, the Yonge Condominium Corridor Association, and various chapters of the Canadian Condominium Institute.

Scott wrote this book, "Residential and Condominium Security in Canada," to share his insights and observations with condominium management professionals. His goal is to help them learn from his extensive experience and education, rather than through tragic incidents. His work aims to equip condominium managers with the knowledge and tools necessary to create safer, more secure living environments for residents.

# INTRODUCTION

Welcome to "Residential and Condominium Security in Canada," a comprehensive guide to safeguarding the residential spaces that so many Canadians call home. This book delves into the multifaceted world of residential & condominium security, addressing the unique challenges and solutions pertinent to high-density living environments. This book can be applied to residential apartment buildings as well as condominium high (and low) rise communities. For this reason, the words "condo" "building", "facility" will be used interchangeably throughout the book.

Residential security is crucial for ensuring the safety, privacy, and peace of mind of residents. As urban centers continue to grow, the need for robust security measures in buildings has become more pressing. This book draws on the expertise of our experience as an industry leader in the condominium/ high rise security field, known for our innovative and comprehensive approaches to condominium security.

Established in 2016, 3D Security Services quickly became a trusted name in the security industry, providing tailored solutions for facilities across Ontario. Their approach is holistic, incorporating crime prevention through environmental design (CPTED), advanced technological solutions, and a highly trained workforce to create secure living environments.

One of the core principles emphasized in this book is the importance of a Physical Protection System (PPS), which must effectively deter, detect, and delay (and then respond to) potential security threats. The PPS should serve as both a physical and psychological barrier to intruders, making it clear that the site is well-protected and not an easy target.

Detection systems need to be in place to quickly identify unauthorized access and alert appropriate personnel, while delay tactics ensure that there is sufficient time to respond to any security breach.

Lastly (and this is an important factor), there must be a timely response to any infractions.

Additionally, this book explores the role of uniformed security services in maintaining a secure environment. Effective security personnel are not just a deterrent to crime but also play a critical role in managing access, monitoring common areas, and providing a sense of safety to residents.

Companies like 3D Security Services highlight the importance of well-trained and motivated security staff who understand the specific needs of condominium communities and residential buildings with the ability to handle various security challenges.

We also delve into the significance of proactive security measures, such as regular security audits and risk assessments, to identify vulnerabilities and implement appropriate solutions before incidents occur. By using a comprehensive security package, condominiums can plan and budget for necessary security upgrades, ensuring that they stay ahead of potential threats and maintain a safe living environment for their residents.

"Residential & Condominium Security in Canada" is your essential guide to understanding and implementing effective security strategies in condominium settings. Through the expertise shared within these pages, you will gain valuable insights into creating a secure and peaceful community for all residents.

# CHAPTER 1

## *Understanding Residential and Condominium Security in Canada*

The importance of robust security measures for condominiums and high rises in Canada cannot be overstated. With the increasing urbanization and density of living spaces, ensuring the safety and security of residents has become a top priority for property managers and condominium boards. In Ontario alone, as of 2024, 1.7 million people live in condominiums. This chapter delves into the critical components of condominium security, including security audits, security master plans, threat and risk assessments, emergency planning, and the proactive evaluation of existing security solutions. As we work our way through this book, we will continually use the words "Condominium", "High-Rise", or "building". In the absence of any specific statement to the contrary, the reader can assume that, as they come across these words, they can be read interchangeably.

## Security Audits (SA)

A security audit (SA) is a comprehensive evaluation of a property's security measures and protocols. It serves as the cornerstone of an effective security strategy by identifying vulnerabilities and providing actionable recommendations for improvement. Security audits typically include an assessment of physical barriers, access controls, surveillance systems, and the performance of security personnel, to name a few. They help in understanding the existing security posture and formulating strategies to mitigate identified risks. The issue that condominiums have experienced in the past is a lack of consistency in what constitutes a security audit. There are many suppliers that offer "free audits" to sell their services. This book would recommend that security audits, to be considered valid, should be completed by those who are trained as security professionals. An example of this training would be the Physical Security Professional (PSP) or Certified Professional (CPP) certifications from ASIS. Additionally, the security audit should be conducted by an impartial, third party that does not have any financial gain from the result of the audit. For instance, asking a security camera installer to conduct a security review of the property may result in recommendations for installing cameras. The manager will then need to decide if the cameras are needed or if the installer is trying to sell a product.

A question that often arises regarding the Free Audits that are offered by public services such as municipal police departments. Our experience with these audits has been mixed, as it is not their core business, and they may have a politicized view on the local crime trends and the threats that are facing the property. Most astute managers in today's environment have a healthy skepticism about free products, specifically when it comes to security and protecting life and property.

**Complete Audit vs. Free Audit: A Comparative Overview**

In our experience, there is a significant gap between the conducting of a free audit vs one that is completed by those whose core business is Security Review. Below are some of the differences we have noted.

1. *Number of Site Visits:* One of the foundational differences lies in the frequency and timing of site visits. Our opinion is that a complete audit involves a minimum of five visits, conducted during various times of the day, including nights, weekends, and weekdays. This ensures a holistic understanding of the property's security needs, accounting for changes in lighting, resident activity, and potential threats at different times, including those deemed high-risk.

   In contrast, a free audit typically consists of a single visit during weekday business hours. This limited approach may overlook critical security vulnerabilities that emerge during off-peak times when residents are most vulnerable.

2. *Risk Rating:* A comprehensive risk rating is one of the hallmarks of a complete audit. This process evaluates vulnerabilities based on their severity and prioritizes recommendations accordingly. For instance, areas with poor lighting or high traffic may be flagged for immediate improvement. This systematic approach helps property managers allocate resources efficiently and address the most critical issues first. More on this topic in our discussions on TRA.

Free audits, on the other hand, often lack a formal risk rating. Without this prioritization, property managers may struggle to implement security upgrades effectively, potentially leaving significant vulnerabilities unaddressed.

3. *Quality of Recommendations:* The depth and precision of recommendations are another key differentiator. A complete audit offers detailed, actionable insights. For example, it might specify, "Only 6 foot-candles of lighting are present in the parking area; this should be increased to 10 foot-candles to meet safety standards." Such specificity allows property managers to take targeted action.

   Conversely, recommendations from a free audit can be vague, such as "need more lighting in the front area." While well-intentioned, these general suggestions may lack the context and data required for effective implementation.

4. *Training and Expertise:* Professional complete audits are conducted by security specialists with extensive training. These experts often complete various security modules, passing rigorous assessments with marks of 80% or higher. Additionally, they are required to engage in continuing education to maintain their certifications and stay updated on industry best practices.

   In contrast, individuals conducting free audits may receive limited CPTED (Crime Prevention Through Environmental Design) training, usually lasting one or two weeks. While this training provides a solid foundation, it may not equip them with the specialized knowledge required for in-depth residential security evaluations.

5. *Depth of Audit:* A complete audit delves deep into the integration of security systems and processes. It examines all the areas that are detailed in this book.

   In contrast, free audits primarily, sometimes exclusively, focus on external areas, such as lighting and environmental factors. While these aspects are important, the lack of attention to internal systems and processes may leave significant gaps in the overall security framework.

6. *Understanding of Condominium & Residential Processes*: Condominiums have unique governance structures and financial restrictions. For example, some expenses must be allocated to reserve funds rather than operating budgets, and changes to common elements often require board approval or a vote from residents. A complete audit takes these factors into account, ensuring that recommendations align with condominium governance policies.

Free audits, however, may not consider these nuances. Without a deep understanding of condominium operations, recommendations might be impractical or non-compliant with governance rules.

The choice between a complete audit and a free audit often boils down to cost versus value. While free audits are a convenient option that check a box, they may provide limited insights and lack the depth needed for a robust security strategy. A complete audit, though requiring an investment, offers unparalleled benefits:

- Tailored Recommendations: Address specific vulnerabilities with precision.

- Comprehensive Risk Assessment: Prioritize issues based on severity.

- Expertise and Training: Leverage the knowledge of highly trained professionals.

- Long-Term Solutions: Ensure security measures comply with governance policies and are sustainable over time.

- By choosing a complete audit, property managers can proactively address security challenges, reduce liability, and enhance the safety and satisfaction of residents.

In an era where residential security is more critical than ever, the value of a comprehensive security audit cannot be overstated. While free audits provide a basic overview, they may fall short in delivering the actionable insights and tailored solutions that condominiums and residential properties require. Investing in a professional complete audit is not just about mitigating risks—it's about fostering a secure, resilient, and well-managed living environment for all. Property managers, board members, and security professionals must recognize the importance of thorough evaluations and commit to audits that provide the depth, precision, and expertise needed to safeguard their communities. When it comes to security, cutting corners should not be an option.

## Threat and Risk Assessments (TRA)

Threat and Risk Assessments (TRAs) are essential reports for identifying potential threats and evaluating the likelihood and impact of those threats on the building and their residents. TRAs involve a detailed analysis of both internal and external risks, such as unauthorized access, criminal activity, and natural disasters. The outcome of a TRA helps in prioritizing security measures and allocating resources effectively to areas of highest risk.

When reviewing a TRA, the property manager should look at both the probability of a threat materializing, the impact of if that threat comes to fruition, and the risk once that threat has occurred. A TRA is useful in prioritizing security vulnerabilities in the building, so that the ones with the most risk may be addressed in a timely manner. For this reason, the templates that are used for security audits often include a section for assigning both probability and impact.

Once this is done, managers can effectively analyze risks to residents and property in the buildings by employing a risk matrix. This involves identifying potential threats and assessing them based on their probability of occurrence and potential impact. The matrix categorizes risks into different levels, assigning them a numeric value, allowing property managers to objectively prioritize actions. For instance, a high-probability, high-impact risk like unauthorized access might necessitate immediate enhanced security measures, while a low-probability, low-impact risk such as minor vandalism may require routine monitoring. This systematic approach ensures that resources are allocated efficiently, enhancing overall safety and security.

When addressing identified risks, property managers have four primary options: accept, mitigate, eliminate, or off-load the risk. Accepting the risk may be appropriate for low-probability, low-impact scenarios where action is unnecessary or cost-prohibitive. Mitigating the risk involves implementing measures to reduce its probability or impact, such as upgrading access control systems or increasing patrols. Eliminating the risk entirely may involve substantial changes, such as permanently securing vulnerable areas to prevent unauthorized access. Off-loading the risk, such as transferring liability through insurance or outsourcing specific security functions, can also be an effective strategy, especially for risks that are difficult to manage directly. These options provide a structured framework for decision-making, ensuring risks are managed in alignment with available resources and organizational goals.

The advantage of the TRA over the SA is that it provides managers with valuable information to take to the decision-makers to obtain the resources required to effect change. With the risk being assigned a numeric value, it makes it easier to recommend a security solution—because it is now objective rather than subjective. This is very important in settings such as condominiums where a manager must convince a majority of the board members (or in the case of a substantial change—potentially 66 2/3 of the owners) to approve the budget required to mitigate or eliminate the risk.

## Security Master Plan (SMP)

A Security Master Plan (SMP) serves as a cornerstone for ensuring the long-term safety and security of residents in condominiums and high-rise buildings. It is a comprehensive, strategic document that outlines the security objectives of a building and integrates the findings from Security Audits (SA) and Threat Risk Assessments (TRA). The SMP is more than just a reactive framework; it is a proactive strategy designed to address both current and future security needs. Despite its importance, few residential buildings currently have a complete SMP, leaving a significant gap in their ability to effectively manage security risks.

An SMP provides a structured and cohesive strategy that ensures all security measures—from access control to surveillance, incident response, and emergency management—align with the overall objectives of the building. The plan is based on comprehensive assessments, including:

- Security Audits: Detailed reviews of existing security measures to identify strengths, weaknesses, and areas for improvement.

- Threat Risk Assessments: Evaluations of potential risks, threats, and vulnerabilities specific to the building and its environment.

The SMP is designed to evolve, adapting to changes in technology, regulations, and the building's operational needs. This adaptability ensures it remains a relevant and practical tool for managing security.

*Why Are SMPs Rarely Implemented?*

At the time of writing, the adoption of SMPs in residential buildings remains limited. The challenges to implementation are multifaceted, with two key issues standing out:

*Convincing Owners of Their Duty of Care:* Building owners have a legal and ethical duty to ensure the safety of their residents. However, many fail to recognize that proactive security planning is the most effective way to fulfill this duty. Without immediate incidents highlighting the need for robust security measures, it can be difficult to persuade owners to invest in a comprehensive SMP.

*Perception of Security Documents as Static:* There is a widespread misconception that security documents are static, one-time efforts. This mindset overlooks the dynamic nature of security risks and the necessity for regular updates to security strategies. Just as condominiums conduct Reserve Fund Studies to plan for future repairs and replacements, SMPs should be treated as living documents, regularly reviewed and revised to remain effective.

## Components of an Effective SMP

A well-designed SMP addresses multiple aspects of security, integrating them into a unified strategy. Key components include:

- Access Control: Policies and procedures for managing who enters the building and under what conditions. This includes:

- Use of secure entry systems such as key fobs or biometric scanners.

- Visitor management processes.

- Protocols for handling unauthorized access attempts.

- Surveillance: A robust surveillance system acts as both a deterrent and a tool for incident investigation.

- Regular maintenance and system upgrades.

- Incident Response: Clear procedures for responding to security incidents, ensuring a swift and coordinated approach. This involves:

  o Training staff and residents on emergency protocols.

  o Establishing communication channels for reporting and managing incidents.

  o Conducting regular drills to test and refine response strategies.

  o Emergency Management: Plans for dealing with crises such as fires, natural disasters, or criminal activities.

The reluctance to adopt SMPs often stems from a combination of cost concerns, lack of awareness, and resistance to change. Addressing these barriers requires a targeted approach:

*Educating Owners and Managers:* Emphasizing the concept of duty of care and the potential legal and financial repercussions of inadequate security can help build support for SMPs. Highlighting case studies of incidents that could have been mitigated with a proactive security strategy can also be persuasive.

*Promoting SMPs as Living Documents:* Drawing parallels with other ongoing building assessments, such as Reserve Fund Studies, can help normalize the concept of regular SMP updates. Demonstrating the long-term cost savings of proactive security—by preventing incidents and reducing liability—can further strengthen the case.

*Leveraging Technology:* The integration of advanced technologies, such as AI-driven surveillance and real-time incident reporting systems, can make SMPs more effective and appealing. Owners and managers are more likely to invest in a plan that incorporates cutting-edge tools and demonstrates tangible benefits.

## The Future of SMPs

As security incidents become more frequent and severe, the demand for comprehensive SMPs is expected to grow. Proactive building owners and managers who adopt SMPs early will not only enhance resident safety but also gain a competitive edge in the market. Over time, regulatory changes may mandate the development and maintenance of SMPs, making it essential for industry stakeholders to prepare now.

A Security Master Plan is an essential tool for managing the complex security needs of condominiums and high-rise buildings. By integrating findings from security audits and threat assessments, an SMP provides a strategic framework that addresses both current vulnerabilities and future risks. Overcoming the challenges of implementation requires a shift in mindset among owners and managers, emphasizing the importance of proactive planning and regular updates. As the industry evolves, SMPs are likely to become a standard practice, ensuring safer and more secure living environments for all residents.

## The Three Categories of Security Solutions

Regularly evaluating and updating security measures is essential for maintaining an effective security posture. This proactive approach involves testing the effectiveness of existing controls, conducting regular security audits and Threat Risk Assessments (TRAs), and staying informed about emerging threats and technologies. By consistently assessing and enhancing security solutions, residential condominiums can stay ahead of potential risks and ensure the safety of their residents.

In building security, solutions can be classified into **Three Categories of Security Solutions**:

1. **Security Staff**

   Security staff provide the most effective solution, offering immediate, human response and intervention. While this option represents the highest cost, it is unparalleled in its ability to quickly assess and react to security threats. Trained professionals are indispensable in high-risk environments, ensuring a level of adaptability and decision-making that technology and policies alone cannot achieve.

2. **Technology and Equipment**

   Falling in the middle ground of cost and effectiveness, technology and equipment enhance security through continuous monitoring and automated responses. This category includes tools such as surveillance cameras, access control systems, and alarms, which collectively bolster a building's security posture. Although they lack the immediacy of human intervention, these technologies provide an essential layer of protection that complements other measures.

3. **Policies and Procedures**

   Policies and procedures are the most cost-effective solution but offer the lowest level of immediate effectiveness. This category encompasses the rules, guidelines, and protocols designed to prevent incidents through regulation and routine. While critical for establishing a structured security framework, their success relies heavily on compliance and enforcement by residents and staff. As such, they often fall short when addressing immediate threats compared to the other two categories.

## Key Security Solutions

The following is a list of the security solutions that most condominiums and high-rise buildings utilize to protect their property and residents. Each one of these security solutions will be explored more fully in their chapter in this book.

## Perimeter Protection

Perimeter protection involves securing the outer boundaries of the condominium property. This can include fencing, gates, and barriers designed to prevent unauthorized access. Effective perimeter protection acts as the first line of defense, deterring potential intruders and providing a clear demarcation of private property. This is of critical importance, as it is the "First Impression" of the security effectiveness of the building.

## Access Control

Access control systems regulate who can enter and exit the building. This includes physical access controls like keycards, biometric scanners, and intercom systems, as well as policies governing visitor access and contractor entry. Access control ensures that only authorized individuals can enter the property, reducing the risk of unauthorized access and potential security breaches.

## Security Lighting

Adequate lighting is a critical component of building security. Security lighting illuminates' dark areas around the property, making it difficult for intruders to hide and enhance the visibility of security cameras. Well-placed lighting can also create a sense of safety for residents and deter criminal activity by increasing the risk of detection.

## Video Camera Systems

Video surveillance is a fundamental aspect of residential condominium security. Security cameras provide real-time monitoring and recording of activities within and around the property. Modern systems offer high-definition video, remote access, and advanced features like motion detection and facial recognition. Effective surveillance systems help in deterring crime, monitoring suspicious activities, and providing evidence in case of incidents.

## Crime Prevention Through Environmental Design (CPTED)

CPTED is a multi-disciplinary approach to deterring criminal behavior through environmental design. It involves the strategic use of landscaping, building design, and public space management to reduce opportunities for crime. CPTED principles include natural surveillance, access control, territorial reinforcement, and maintenance. By creating an environment that is unattractive to criminals, buildings can enhance their overall security. This book will also discuss the first generation CPTED, which is physical components, as well as the second generation, which deals with social cohesion. Finally, we will introduce 3rd Gen CPTED.

## Security Staff

Trained security personnel play a vital role in maintaining the safety and security of any building. Security staff are responsible for monitoring access points, conducting patrols, responding to incidents, and aiding residents and visitors. Effective security staffing requires ongoing training and performance evaluations to ensure that personnel are equipped to handle various security challenges

**Emergency Planning**

Emergency planning involves preparing for potential incidents that could compromise the safety and security of the buildings. This includes developing and regularly updating emergency response plans, conducting drills, and ensuring that all residents and staff are aware of their roles during an emergency. Effective emergency planning can significantly reduce the impact of incidents and enhance the overall resilience of the condominium. In addition, Emergency training with the staff (superintendent, cleaners, security, concierge, managers, etc.) will increase both the confidence of the team and identify any gaps in the plan. There is a section on different training drills / methodologies in the Security Staff chapter.

**The Pillars of Emergency Management and Their Application to Residential Condominiums**

Emergency management is a structured approach that aims to protect communities from the impacts of disasters and emergencies. Examples of the pillars of emergency management that may be implemented into residential buildings include Prevention, Mitigation, Response, and Recovery. These pillars can form a comprehensive framework for dealing with emergencies in various settings, including high rise buildings and condominiums. Here's how these pillars (with some examples) may apply to these buildings:

1. **Prevention** involves actions taken to avoid or stop an emergency before it occurs. In the context of high rises or condominiums, this can include measures such as:

   o Implementing strict security protocols to prevent unauthorized access.

   o Conduct regular inspections to identify and address potential hazards, such as faulty cameras or lack of key control.

   o Educating residents on safe practices to reduce the risk of fires, floods, and other emergencies.

2. **Mitigation** involves efforts to reduce the impact of disasters that cannot be prevented. In high rise & condominiums, this could be achieved through:

   o Ensuring the buildings have contingencies / detection in the event of power outages, occupations, etc.

   o Using flood detection devices and/or regular physical inspections to minimize water damage.

   o Implement an on-going budget to help cover costs related to emergencies and repairs.

   o Regularly (annually) reviewing insurance policies to ensure that disasters are covered, and risks are mitigated to the lowest level.

3. **Response:** includes immediate actions taken during and after an emergency to protect lives and property. For building communities, effective response strategies include:

   o Developing and practicing emergency response plans that cover a range of scenarios.

   o Establishing communication systems to quickly disseminate information to residents during an emergency. This should be done both during an emergency (activation) and following the event (termination).

   o Training staff and residents in first aid, CPR, and basic emergency response techniques. This is a WSIB requirement.

4. **Recovery** focuses on restoring the community to its pre-disaster state and improving resilience against future incidents. Recovery efforts in residential condominiums might involve:

   o Coordinating with insurance companies and contractors to expedite repairs and reconstruction.

- ○ Providing support services for affected residents, such as temporary housing and mental health resources.

- ○ Reviewing and updating emergency plans based on lessons learned from the incident to enhance future preparedness.

By integrating these pillars into their emergency management strategies, condominiums and residential buildings can create a safer environment for their residents and ensure they are well-prepared to handle emergencies. This comprehensive approach not only protects lives and property, but also fosters a sense of security and resilience within the community.

## Risks of Inaction

Neglecting proper security measures in condominium buildings can lead to severe consequences, including legal action, financial losses, and harm to residents.

## Conclusion and Key Takeaways

The safety and security of residents in condominiums and high-rise buildings are paramount in ensuring a stable and peaceful living environment. As urbanization continues to rise, the importance of adopting robust security measures has never been more critical. This chapter has provided an overview of the foundational elements of condominium security, including security audits, threat and risk assessments, security master plans, and the pillars of emergency management.

By addressing vulnerabilities proactively and adopting a structured approach, property managers and boards can prioritize the safety of their residents, mitigate risks, and avoid costly consequences. Ignoring security measures is not only a dereliction of duty but can also lead to financial, legal, and reputational harm.

**Key Takeaways:**

1. **Security Audits and TRAs:**

   o Security audits should be impartial and conducted by certified professionals (e.g., PSP or CPP) to ensure validity and actionable insights.

   o Threat and Risk Assessments (TRAs) provide a systematic method to evaluate risks, prioritize actions, and advocate for necessary resources objectively.

2. **Security Master Plans:**

   o Developing and maintaining a Security Master Plan ensures a comprehensive, long-term strategy that adapts to emerging threats and technologies.

   o These plans must be treated as living documents, updated regularly, and integrated into the building's overall management practices.

3. **Three Categories of Security Solutions:**

   o Security staff, technology, and policies each offer unique benefits, with their effectiveness dependent on their integration and alignment with the building's specific needs.

4. **Emergency Management:**

   o Prevention, mitigation, response, and recovery form the pillars of emergency management, ensuring that buildings are prepared for and resilient against emergencies.

   o Training and collaboration among staff, residents, and external partners are crucial for a robust emergency response.

5. **Risks of Inaction:**

   ○ Neglecting security can result in severe legal, financial, and reputational consequences. Real-world examples underline the importance of proactive maintenance and implementation of security measures.

## Looking Ahead

The subsequent chapters will delve deeper into individual security components and solutions, offering practical guidance and case studies. By building on the foundation laid in this chapter, property managers and condominium boards will be equipped to create safer, more secure communities that adapt to modern challenges and enhance resident satisfaction.

# CHAPTER 2

## *Perimeter Protection*

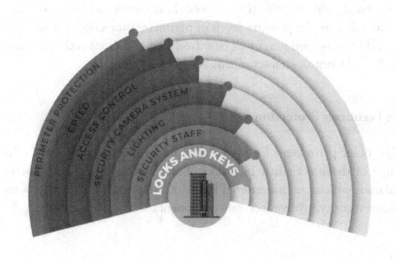

## Introduction

A property's perimeter protection must be evaluated in its ability to delay, deter, or detect would-be intruders from accessing the property. The earlier that this goal is achieved, the better for the security of the property. The security concept of **Protection in Depth** (or layered security) advocates layers of security around the asset which, in this case, is the building's residents and their property. As the layers move in towards the asset, the security gets tighter. This is illustrated in the diagram on the title page of this chapter. This chapter will explore these layers, focusing on the primary levels of perimeter protection: Outer. The Inner and Internal perimeter will be introduced and discussed more fully in the Access Control chapter of this book.

## Outer Perimeter Protection

The outer perimeter of a high rise building or condominium is the first line of defense against intruders. This includes the civic property boundaries, which are the external limits of the property. Effective outer perimeter security involves several components.

## Gatehouse (s)

For condominiums fortunate enough to have a gatehouse, this essential security feature can significantly enhance resident safety and peace of mind—provided it is used effectively. A gatehouse is more than just a checkpoint; it is the first line of defense against unauthorized access and a vital part of the condominium's overall security infrastructure. However, simply having a gatehouse is not enough. To truly maximize its value, condominiums must implement robust procedures to ensure that visitors and contractors are properly vetted and logged.

A well-managed gatehouse serves as the control center for monitoring and regulating access to the property. It is the point where residents, visitors, and service personnel intersect with security protocols. Gatehouse staff, often security guards, play a critical role in maintaining a secure environment. Their responsibilities include verifying identities, recording entries and exits, and addressing any suspicious behavior or potential threats. However, these responsibilities must be supported by clear policies and proper training. Without them, the gatehouse risks becoming a weak link in the condominium's security chain.

Residents must also play an active role in supporting gatehouse operations. Encouraging them to report suspicious activity, adhere to visitor notification procedures, and cooperate with gatehouse staff fosters a culture of security throughout the community.

## Signage

Signage plays a crucial role in deterrence. At the boundaries of the property, there should be clear signs indicating that the property is private, is under surveillance (if true), and that there is no trespassing on the property. These signs can significantly deter potential intruders. The best security practices dictate that signage should be placed at all entrances and exits. This not only helps in legally charging trespassers, should it be necessary, but also reinforces the message that unauthorized access is not permitted (sets the tone of security). Additionally, adding signage in magnet locations (locations that draw unwanted activities), such as staircases, where trespassers are likely to migrate to, can further enhance security.

## Enhancing Surveillance Signage

To maximize the deterrent effect, condominiums may consider posting additional signage indicating that the property is patrolled by a security company. This can be particularly effective in high-traffic areas and near entrances and exits. Clear, visible signs stating that the property is monitored by security personnel can significantly reduce the likelihood of unauthorized access. As an added measure, building may post signage asking residents to report any security concerns to a website, security team, or concierge staff. This is an example of 2nd generation CPTED, where residents are empowered to participate in the effective safety of the building. To achieve proper results from this security measure, managers are cautioned to ensure that if concerns are reported, they are acted upon, and the resident receives a response. Failure to do so will reinforce the residents' belief that managers are non-responsive and do not care about them or their building.

## Barriers

Physical barriers are another essential component of outer perimeter protection. In many condominiums, decorative fencing defines the property lines. However, for effective security, this fencing needs to be robust and continuous. Most fencing, although aesthetically pleasing, is inadequate due to its low height and discontinuities (openings). If used as a security barrier, it is recommended that the condominium consider installing a fence at least 6 feet high with an additional 1-foot header. This fence should surround the entire property, with gated entrances and exits. Most buildings that 3D Security has audited do not have a "security fence" but many have a fence. This does not render them useless from a security perspective. If the building does not have a sufficient height fence to be considered a security banner, they can act as a deterrent and can be used to implement territorial reinforcement (CPTED). Additionally, there are other methods that can be used to increase their effectiveness, such as the incorporation of hostile vegetation.

## Hostile Vegetation as a Security Barrier

An innovative and increasingly popular approach to enhancing the perimeter protection of a high-rise building is the use of hostile vegetation as a security barrier. This method not only enhances physical security, but also contributes to the aesthetic appeal and environmental sustainability of the property.

## The Concept of Hostile Vegetation

Hostile vegetation refers to the strategic planting of thorny, dense, and tough plants that create a natural barrier, deterring unauthorized access. These plants are selected for their physical characteristics, which makes it difficult and uncomfortable for intruders to pass through. Common examples include:

- **Roses:** Known for their beauty and thorny stems, roses can form an attractive yet formidable barrier.

- **Holly:** With its sharp, spiky leaves, holly is an evergreen option that remains effective year-round.

- **Barberry:** This shrub features dense branches with sharp thorns, making it an excellent deterrent.

- **Bougainvillea:** While visually appealing with its vibrant flowers, bougainvillea has robust thorns that can deter intruders.

## Advantages of Hostile Vegetation

1. **Aesthetic Appeal:** Unlike traditional barriers, hostile vegetation enhances the landscape design, providing a visually pleasing environment for residents.

2. **Environmental Benefits:** These plants contribute to the local ecosystem, supporting wildlife and promoting biodiversity.

3. **Cost-Effective:** Once established, hostile vegetation requires minimal maintenance compared to fences or walls, reducing long-term security costs.

4. **Discreet Security:** Hostile vegetation blends seamlessly into the environment, offering a subtle yet effective security solution.

## Implementation Strategies

To maximize the effectiveness of hostile vegetation as a security barrier, the following strategies should be considered:

1. **Strategic Placement:** Identify vulnerable areas around the property's perimeter where hostile vegetation can be most effective. Focus on points of entry, such as low fences, walls, and ground-level windows.

2. **Layered Approach:** Combine hostile vegetation with other security measures like fences, lighting, and surveillance cameras to create a multi-layered defense system.

3. **Maintenance Plan:** Regularly trim and care for the vegetation to ensure it remains dense and impassable. Address any gaps that may develop over time.

4. **Resident Education:** Inform residents about the purpose and benefits of hostile vegetation. Encourage them to report any breaches or damage to the plants.

## Challenges and Considerations

While hostile vegetation offers numerous benefits, it is essential to consider potential challenges:

- **Initial Cost and Effort:** Establishing a hostile vegetation barrier requires an initial investment in plants and labor for planting.

- **Growth Time:** Unlike immediate solutions like fences, plants take time to grow and become effective barriers.

- **Maintenance:** Regular maintenance is necessary to ensure the vegetation remains an effective deterrent.

- **Safety Concerns:** Ensure that the placement of hostile vegetation does not pose a risk to residents, particularly children and pets.

## Inner Perimeter Protection

The inner perimeter of a high-rise building usually encompasses the structural building envelope, including the parking garage, buildings walls, doors, and windows. Securing these areas will be addressed in detail under the Access Control section of this report. However, it is important to note that effective inner perimeter security relies on a combination of physical barriers, surveillance, and controlled access points.

## Detection - Surveillance

Surveillance is an important component of perimeter protection. Effective use of cameras on the outer boundaries can detect potential intruders and provide more time for security response to form. As previously noted, signage should be posted advising pedestrians and others that the building is under video surveillance and that trespassers will be prosecuted. This will be discussed more fully in the Video Surveillance System section of this book.

## Lighting

Adequate lighting is essential for effective perimeter and ground security. Well-lit areas (such as courtyards, loading bays, stairwell door exits, etc.) are less attractive to intruders and provide better visibility for surveillance cameras. High Rise building & Condominiums should ensure that all entrances, exits, and pathways are well lit. Motion-activated lights can be particularly effective in conserving energy while providing security only when needed. If the areas with motion sensors are monitored by cameras, they can also be used to alert security when a person enters this area.

## Landscaping

Landscaping can either enhance or detract from perimeter security. Dense shrubbery and trees can provide cover for intruders, while well-maintained, open landscaping can improve visibility and reduce hiding spots. The residential buildings should consider landscaping strategies that promote visibility and deter unauthorized access – utilizing the CPTED concept of Natural Surveillance. For example, as previously mentioned, planting thorny bushes near fences can act as a natural barrier, while maintaining clear lines of sight for surveillance cameras can improve monitoring. This issue is discussed more fully in the CPTED section of this book.

## Access Control

Access control is a critical component of both inner and internal perimeter security. Effective access control measures include:

**Controlled Entry Points:** All entry points to the property, including pedestrian and vehicle entrances, should be controlled. This can be achieved using gates, keys, and/or access card (fob) systems. Ensuring that only authorized individuals can enter the building is essential for maintaining security.

**Visitor Management:** A robust visitor management system can help track who is entering and leaving the property. Visitors and contractors should be required to sign in and out, and their access should be logged and limited to specific areas of the property that they are required to access. Implementing an online visitor management system that logs both visitors and contractors can speed up this process and provide better auditing and reporting.

## Conclusion & Takeaways

Perimeter protection forms the foundation of a comprehensive security strategy for high-rise buildings and condominiums. By implementing layered security measures—outer, inner, and internal—properties can effectively deter, delay, and detect potential intrusions, enhancing the safety and comfort of residents.

Key takeaways from this chapter include:

1. **Protection in Depth:** Adopting a layered security approach strengthens the overall defense of the property by creating multiple barriers that intruders must overcome to reach their target.

2. **Outer Perimeter Protection:**

   o Signage: Clear and visible signage deters intruders, supports legal enforcement, and empowers residents to participate in security.

   o Barriers and Hostile Vegetation: Fencing, combined with strategic landscaping using thorny plants, can act as an effective physical and visual deterrent while maintaining aesthetic appeal.

3. **Surveillance and Lighting:** The strategic use of surveillance cameras and motion-activated lighting enhances detection and discourages unauthorized access.

4. **Inner Perimeter Protection:**

   o Access Control: Controlled entry points and robust visitor management systems are essential for maintaining the integrity of the property.

   o Landscaping: Thoughtful landscaping enhances visibility and natural surveillance while reducing potential hiding spots.

5. **Resident Engagement:** Incorporating 2nd generation CPTED principles encourages residents to report security concerns, fostering a collaborative and proactive security culture.

By integrating these practices, managers and security teams can create a secure and welcoming environment that meets the needs of residents while adapting to evolving security challenges.

# CHAPTER 3

## *Access Control*

Effective access control is a critical element of residential security. Access control is defined as a security system designed to allow the movement of authorized personnel and materials through normal access routes while detecting and/or delaying unauthorized personnel and materials from entering or exiting the protected area—in this case, the building complex and its common elements.

During physical security inspections, the procedures and equipment in place to detect, delay, or deter potential intruders attempting to access the property improperly should be evaluated and assessed for effectiveness. Additionally, limited penetration testing should be conducted to determine the ease with which security solutions could be breached.

Control of access to a building can be managed by one of three processes, or a combination of these processes: access can be granted through something a person has (e.g., key, fob), something they know (e.g., access code, password), or something they are (e.g., fingerprint, retinal scan, voice print). The stricter the security requirements are for the facility; the more controls and combinations are put in place.

As mentioned in the previous chapter on Perimeter Protection, the building boundaries are considered the inner boundary of protecting the facility. Due diligence must be provided to ensure that the inner boundaries (building envelope) are protected. To best protect the residents and their property, access control procedures and equipment (as well as the training and awareness of personnel) must be properly implemented. This counters any architectural limitations of securing the outer boundary (such as low fences or access through public facilities such as a public garage or commercial unit).

## Key Management and Vulnerabilities

Master and unit keys are critical assets whose compromise poses significant risks to the condominium. If a key is lost or stolen, the corporation may be liable for any resulting incidents. Court cases in the United States have held condominiums civilly responsible for tragic outcomes stemming from improperly secured access. Additionally, the building could incur significant costs if forced to re-key the building due to a lost master key.

During any security audit or risk assessment the issuing and storing of any master or unit keys should be thoroughly investigated and tested for weakness. The importance of having back-up security protection (layers) around the keys to the units cannot be overstated, as tragic results could stem from them falling into the wrong hands. Key cabinets should be protected by at least 2 systems, such as being locked and under video surveillance, or being in a secured office with motion sensors that need to be deactivated upon entering. In addition, the process in which a master key may be removed should be examined to ensure that there is a proper audit of its usage. The presence of a master key should be confirmed and documented on a regular basis to prevent missing keys from not being addressed.

## Tailgating

Tailgating, or "piggybacking," is one of the most frequent methods intruders use to bypass access control measures in condominium properties. This security breach occurs when an unauthorized individual closely follows an authorized person into a secured area without using their own credentials. While tailgating might seem harmless at first glance, it poses significant risks, including theft, vandalism, and endangering the safety of residents.

### Why Is Tailgating So Common?

1.  **Human Behavior**: Many residents are reluctant to challenge someone they perceive as a stranger, fearing confrontation or appearing rude. This hesitation is natural and stems from societal norms emphasizing politeness.

2.  **Design Flaws**: Buildings with poorly designed entry points, such as doors that remain open for an extended period or multiple access points, make tailgating easier.

3.  **Lack of Awareness**: Residents may not fully understand the security risks associated with tailgating or the potential consequences of allowing unauthorized access. In some cases, we have watched well-meaning residents hold the door open for non-residents.

**Challenges in Addressing Tailgating**

1. **Resident Reluctance:** Asking residents to confront potential tailgaters directly can create discomfort and even risk escalation if the intruder becomes aggressive.

2. **Education Gaps:** Without proper education, residents may not recognize the importance of denying access or the appropriate steps to take when they observe tailgating.

3. **Physical Barriers:** While access control systems such as key fobs, card readers, or biometric scanners are effective, they cannot prevent tailgating if unauthorized individuals follow too closely.

**Solutions: Education and Design**

Addressing tailgating requires a multifaceted approach that combines education, design improvements, and community engagement.

1. **Resident Education and Awareness**

   • **Regular Communication:** Use newsletters, posters, and digital platforms to remind residents about the dangers of tailgating and the importance of vigilance.

   • **Workshops and Seminars:** Host security awareness sessions to educate residents on recognizing suspicious behavior and safely responding to potential threats.

   • **Reporting Mechanisms:** Encourage residents to report tailgating incidents to management immediately or contact the police in emergencies. Establish anonymous reporting channels to make it easier for residents to come forward.

2. **Social Cohesion and Resident Empowerment**

   • **Foster a Security-Conscious Community:** Encourage residents to get to know their neighbors, which can help identify unfamiliar individuals more easily.

- **Empower Residents to Act:** While direct confrontation is not always advisable, residents should feel confident in reporting suspicious behavior to building management or security staff.

3. **Physical and Technological Measures**

- **Access Control Enhancements:** Install intercom systems or video cameras at entry points to verify visitors before granting access.

- **Surveillance Systems:** Position cameras to monitor entry points, providing an additional layer of deterrence and evidence collection.

## Integrating CPTED Principles

Crime Prevention Through Environmental Design (CPTED) plays a critical role in addressing tailgating. Strategies like improving lighting, ensuring clear sightlines around entrances, and using signage to deter unauthorized access can significantly reduce opportunities for tailgating. Moreover, CPTED's emphasis on social cohesion and community participation aligns with fostering a culture of shared responsibility for security.

Addressing tailgating is a collaborative effort that requires proactive measures, from educating residents to enhancing building design and access control systems. By prioritizing awareness, leveraging technology, and fostering a sense of community, property managers can significantly reduce the risks associated with tailgating and create a safer living environment for all residents.

This topic will be explored in greater depth in the **CPTED Chapter**, focusing on Social Cohesion and Resident Empowerment as essential elements of a comprehensive security strategy.

## Lockbox Security

One of the crime trends in building security is condominiums and high-rise buildings are frequently targeted by thieves who compromised building security by stealing or destroying lockboxes and accessing the keys inside. In some instances, lockboxes are pried off walls and taken to other locations to be broken into; in other situations, they were opened with simple tools like a hammer and chisel on the spot. To combat this vulnerability, buildings such as condominiums must ensure that lockboxes are protected and not stored in locations that facilitate crime (i.e. "deep in the shadows"). The "natural surveillance" concept of Crime Prevention through Environmental Design (CPTED) would dictate that lockboxes should be in plain sight (natural surveillance) and under video surveillance. In addition, lockboxes should be registered with management and regularly checked by staff members (Security, Superintendent, cleaners, etc.). As one of our recommendations from security audits, we always recommend that condominiums should assign a time limit on realtor lockboxes, after which they should be removed. Of course, any missing lockboxes would be a potential security risk and should be investigated immediately.

If lockboxes are not allowed due to the rules or bylaws of the condominium, it is recommended that the property be checked regularly (at least weekly) to ensure they are removed from the site and not installed without the building's knowledge. It is truly amazing how cunning people can be to sneak lockboxes on or around a site that prohibits them.

## Access Control - Technological Integration

Modern access control systems often integrate various technologies to enhance security. These can include:

- **Electronic Key Cards and Fobs**: These provide a convenient and secure way for residents to access the building and common areas. Lost or stolen cards can be quickly deactivated. This is an example of the "something you have"

- **Biometric Systems**: Fingerprint, retinal, or facial recognition ("something you are") systems add a high level of security by ensuring that only authorized individuals can gain access. Although these are not common in high rise buildings (yet), condos and others will sometimes use punch code locks in some of the common elements ("something you know").

- **Intercom Systems**: These allow residents to verify the identity of visitors before granting access, enhancing security and control over who enters the building. Two common mistakes that we see with intercom systems in high rise buildings and condominiums are:

  o Not changing the default password of the software

  o Not changing the lock of the system to one unique to the building.

## Garage Doors

Garage doors are a critical component of residential security, as they often serve as a primary entry point for vehicles and potential intruders. Properties should prioritize the installation of high-security, quick-closing garage doors to minimize the window of opportunity for unauthorized access. These doors should be configured to remain open only as long as necessary for vehicles to enter or exit. Residents must also be educated to remain vigilant, ensuring they do not drive away until the door has fully closed behind them. Additionally, regular monitoring and maintenance of the door's open-close timing are essential to prevent vulnerabilities caused by malfunctions or delays. By implementing these measures, properties can significantly reduce the risks associated with garage door access and enhance overall building security.

## Regular Audits of Fobs, Master Keys, and Garage Remotes

Residential buildings, particularly condominiums and apartment complexes, often rely on electronic fobs, master keys, and garage remotes to manage access. These tools are critical for ensuring residents' safety, protecting property, and maintaining the smooth operation of the building. However, their effectiveness depends on how well they are managed and monitored – as the saying goes "Garbage In – Garbage Out". This applies to the fob database. Conducting regular audits of these access tools is not just a best practice—it is an essential component of a comprehensive security strategy.

## Why Regular Audits Are Necessary

1. *Prevent Unauthorized Access:* Fobs, master keys, and garage remotes grant significant access to a building. If these items fall into the wrong hands due to loss, theft, or misuse, they can compromise security. Regular audits help identify missing or unaccounted-for items promptly, reducing the risk of unauthorized access.

2. *Maintain an Accurate Inventory Over time:* Residential buildings experience turnover as tenants or owners move in and out. If fobs or remotes are not returned, or if master keys are duplicated without proper authorization, the inventory of access tools can quickly become inaccurate. An audit ensures that the building has an up-to-date record of all issued items.

3. *Enhance Resident Safety:* Residents expect their building to provide a secure living environment. A lapse in managing access tools could lead to breaches that endanger residents. Audits reinforce the building's commitment to safety and demonstrate proactive management.

4. *Comply with Legal and Insurance Requirements:* In some jurisdictions, landlords or condominium boards have a legal obligation to ensure the security of their property. Regular audits can also meet insurance requirements, potentially reducing liability and ensuring coverage in case of a claim related to unauthorized access.

5. *Identify System Weaknesses:* Audits often reveal vulnerabilities in the system, such as outdated access logs, insufficient tracking procedures, or over-reliance on physical keys instead of electronic systems. Identifying these weaknesses allows building managers to implement improvements.

## Steps for Conducting an Effective Audit

Establish a clear policy outlining the frequency and scope of audits. Ideally, audits should occur at least every year, with additional audits conducted after significant events, such as tenant turnover or security incidents.

Use a Centralized Access Management System. Modern access control systems often include software that tracks issued fobs, remotes, and keys. Utilize this technology to maintain detailed records, including who has been issued which access tool and when.

Verify physical items by conducting a physical check of all master keys and unissued fobs and remotes. Compare the actual inventory to the records in the access management system.

Review access logs. Most access systems generate logs that show when and where fobs or remotes were used. Review these logs to identify unusual patterns, such as repeated failed access attempts or entries during high risk / unauthorized (in the case of a common element) hours.

Notify residents of the audit process and request them to confirm possession of their assigned access tools. This step not only helps account for missing items but also fosters transparency and trust between management and residents.

If a fob, remote, or master key is found to be missing, take immediate action. This might involve deactivating the lost item, reprogramming the system, or rekeying locks to maintain security.

Create a detailed report of the audit, including discrepancies, actions taken, and any recommendations for system improvements. Share this report with the property owner or condominium board.

**Benefits of Regular Audits**

When residents see their building management taking proactive steps to ensure security, it boosts their confidence in the system. This trust is particularly important in fostering a sense of community.

Addressing security issues proactively through audits is often more cost-effective than dealing with the aftermath of a security breach. For example, replacing a master key system after a security incident can be significantly more expensive than preventing the incident through regular audits.

Regular audits promote a culture of security awareness among building staff and residents. When everyone understands the importance of managing access tools responsibly, the overall security posture of the building improves.

**Overcoming Common Challenges**

- Some residents may see audits as intrusive or inconvenient. To address this, communicate the purpose and benefits of audits clearly and ensure the process is as unobtrusive as possible.

- Audits can be time-consuming, especially in larger buildings. Investing in technology, such as digital access systems and automated tracking, can streamline the process and reduce the burden on staff.

- Without a standardized policy, audits can become sporadic and ineffective. Commit to a regular schedule and involve all stakeholders in adhering to the audit plan.

In today's world, where safety and security are paramount, residential building managers cannot afford to overlook the importance of access control. Regular audits of fobs, master keys, and garage remotes ensure that these essential tools are accounted for and functioning as intended. By preventing unauthorized access, maintaining accurate inventories, and enhancing resident safety, these audits serve as a cornerstone of effective property management. Ultimately, a well-executed audit process demonstrates a commitment to security, builds trust with residents, and mitigates risks, creating a safer environment for all.

## VETTING VISITORS and CONTRACTORS

Security and accountability are crucial elements of property management. Property managers play a pivotal role in ensuring the safety and well-being of residents, tenants, and guests. One of the most critical aspects of their role is vetting visitors and contractors to the property and maintaining detailed records of these entries. This process not only safeguards the physical property but also protects its inhabitants and enhances the overall management of the premises. This section explores the importance of vetting visitors and contractors, the benefits of maintaining accurate records, and best practices for implementing a robust visitor management system.

The primary reason for vetting visitors and contractors is to enhance the security of the property. Unauthorized individuals can pose significant risks, ranging from theft and vandalism to personal harm to residents or employees. By ensuring that only authorized persons gain access to the property, property managers can create a safer environment.

For contractors, vetting is essential to verify credentials, insurance, and professional qualifications. This ensures that only reliable and reputable service providers are permitted to work on-site. Similarly, for visitors, whether they are delivery personnel, guests, or vendors, confirming their legitimacy helps prevent potential security breaches.

Effective visitor and contractor management minimizes the risk of unauthorized access. By implementing a system where individuals must identify themselves, state their purpose, and receive approval before entering, property managers can significantly reduce vulnerabilities. Unauthorized individuals who gain access through negligence or oversight can exploit security gaps, causing damage or harm that might otherwise have been avoided.

Maintaining a record of visitors and contractors provides property managers with a detailed account of who was on-site, when they were there, and for what purpose. This information is invaluable in cases of disputes, accidents, or criminal investigations.

When an incident occurs—be it theft, damage, or a safety violation—having a comprehensive record of entries and exits helps property managers identify potential suspects or witnesses. This can expedite investigations and provide law enforcement with crucial leads. In many jurisdictions, property managers are legally required to maintain certain records for insurance and compliance purposes. Failing to document the presence of contractors or visitors could expose property managers to liability if an incident occurs. For instance, if an unvetted contractor causes property damage or injury, the property manager could face legal repercussions for failing to ensure the individual's qualifications or coverage.

A well-managed visitor and contractor system fosters trust among residents. When they see that their property manager is vigilant about who enters the building, they feel reassured that their safety and privacy are a top priority. This sense of security can improve tenant satisfaction and retention, which is crucial for the long-term success of any residential or commercial property.

Residents are more likely to complain if they perceive that unauthorized individuals can easily enter their building. Common concerns include package theft, noise disturbances, and damage to common areas. A robust visitor and contractor vetting process addresses these concerns, demonstrating that management is proactive in safeguarding the property.

Maintaining a record of visitors and contractors also improves operational efficiency. Property managers can use these records to monitor patterns, track service delivery timelines, and assess the performance of contractors. This data can inform decisions, such as selecting preferred vendors or adjusting security protocols. By pre-registering frequent visitors or trusted contractors, property managers can create a seamless access process that balances security with convenience. This reduces delays at the point of entry while maintaining accountability.

Records of contractor visits can help property managers monitor maintenance schedules, ensuring timely completion of repairs or renovations. This reduces the likelihood of service disruptions and associated inconveniences for residents.

As the nature of security threats evolves, property managers must adapt their strategies. Cybersecurity, for instance, has become a critical concern, particularly in properties that use digital access systems. Vetting visitors and contractors include ensuring they understand and adhere to cybersecurity protocols, such as safeguarding access codes or passwords.

Modern visitor management systems (VMS) streamline the vetting and record-keeping process. These systems use tools like ID scanning, digital registration forms, and automated alerts to simplify and enhance security. Property managers can integrate VMS with surveillance systems and access controls to create a holistic security network. Some helpful guidelines are shared below:

- Establish Clear Policies: Create a visitor and contractor policy that outlines the vetting process, including identification requirements, approval procedures, and restrictions on access.

- Use Technology: Leverage tools like visitor management software to digitize records, streamline the check-in process, and ensure data accuracy.

- Pre-Screen Contractors: Verify licenses, insurance, and references before allowing contractors on-site. Maintain an approved vendor list for regular services.

- Train Staff: Ensure that front desk or security personnel are trained in the vetting process and understand the importance of maintaining accurate records.

- Monitor Compliance: Periodically review records and procedures to ensure compliance with policies and legal requirements.

- Communicate with Residents: Inform residents about the visitor and contractor policy, emphasizing its role in enhancing their safety and privacy.

- Regular Audits: Conduct regular audits of visitor and contractor logs to identify discrepancies or patterns that may require further investigation.

## The Role of Documentation

Documentation is the backbone of effective visitor and contractor management. Accurate records provide a timeline of events, create a sense of accountability, and serve as evidence in disputes or investigations.

## What to Record:

- Name and contact details of the visitor or contractor.

- Purpose of the visit

- Time and date of entry and exit

- Vehicle details, if applicable

- Any identification or documentation provided.

## Ensuring Data Security

Given the sensitive nature of this information, property managers must ensure that records are stored securely. Access to these records should be restricted to authorized personnel, and data should be protected against breaches or unauthorized access.

Vetting visitors and contractors and maintaining comprehensive records are fundamental responsibilities of property managers. These practices enhance security, foster trust among residents, and provide a solid foundation for operational efficiency and legal compliance. As threats evolve, property managers must adopt modern tools and strategies to stay ahead, ensuring the safety and integrity of their properties. By implementing robust visitor and contractor management policies, property managers can demonstrate their commitment to safeguarding the community they serve, creating a secure and well-managed environment for all.

**Staff Training and Resident Awareness**

Effective access control relies not only on technology, but also on the awareness and cooperation of residents and staff. Regular education sessions (townhall or newsletters) should be conducted to educate all building occupants on the importance of security protocols and how to identify and report suspicious activity. This includes:

- **Reporting Procedures**: Clear guidelines on how and when to report security concerns. In order to be effective, management must follow up on these concerns or else residents will deem them a waste of time and stop reporting them.

- **Visitor Management**: Policies on handling visitors, deliveries, moves and contractors. In residential buildings, residents moving in and out of the building is a security vulnerability. More and more buildings are implementing rules or procedures that have a guard securing the area during the move.

- **Food Delivery**: There has been considerable concern at the time of publishing about delivery personnel being allowed free access to the building. This book shares this concern and would recommend that buildings implement a policy where residents meet their deliveries at the front door.

- **Emergency Protocols**: As part of the Emergency Plan, steps to take in case of a security breach or other emergency. Recently, we have seen tragic results from security staff not being fully trained in Emergency Plans and the location of emergency equipment such as an annunciator.

This is usually a topic that can be discussed during Annual General Meetings, or by posting in any condominium newsletters. By fostering a community that values and understands security, the overall effectiveness of access control measures is significantly enhanced. As mentioned previously, this empowers the residents to feel more secure in their home, and to become an active participant in its safety. An additional win for the building owners is the logical step that residents that feel valued will take better care of the building, lowering maintenance costs.

## Understanding Fail-Safe and Fail-Secure Mechanisms

In the realm of security for residential buildings such as condominiums, two locking concepts often cause confusion and concern: fail-safe and fail-secure mechanisms. These terms describe the behavior of security systems, particularly electronic locks, during power failures or system malfunctions. Understanding the differences between these mechanisms is essential for managers, superintendents, board members, and security professionals to make informed decisions about their security infrastructure. This will form a part of any discussion during the Emergency Action Plan (EAP) discussion. In years past, a fail-safe system was often used to argue against the move from a physical key system to a much more secure fob system. A lack of understanding of the settings resulted in some buildings being scared that, in the event of a power outage, the front doors would lock, sealing everyone inside or locking them out. Conversely, they would also worry that they would be frozen open, allowing unrestricted access to the entire building. This is a case of a lack of understanding and education will interfere with security progress within the building. A basic understanding of these two systems will allow management to make informed decisions and work those decisions into the EAP.

## Fail-Safe Mechanisms

A fail-safe mechanism is designed to default to a safe condition in the event of a power failure or system malfunction. For electronic locks, this means that the lock will unlock when the power is lost. The primary advantage of fail-safe mechanisms is ensuring safety and access. During emergencies such as fires, ensuring that residents can exit the building quickly and safely is paramount. Fail-safe locks align with fire safety regulations and codes, which often require that doors remain unlockable from the inside to allow for rapid evacuation of the building.

**Pros:**

1. **Enhanced Safety:** Ensures that residents and visitors can exit the building in an emergency, even if there is a power failure.

2. **Compliance with Fire Codes:** Meets fire safety requirements that mandate doors must be unlockable from the inside during emergencies.

3. **Peace of Mind:** Provides reassurance that in the event of a power outage, residents won't be trapped inside the building.

**Cons:**

1. **Security Risk:** In the event of a power failure, doors unlock, potentially allowing unauthorized access. This can be offset in the EAP by assigning staff to control access in the event of a power loss.

2. **Vulnerability to Tampering:** Malicious actors might exploit the fail-safe mechanism by deliberately cutting power to gain access. This can be offset by incorporating the entry system into the emergency backup power systems, such as battery backs or generators.

**Fail-Secure Mechanisms**

Conversely, a fail-secure mechanism defaults to a secure condition when power is lost. For electronic locks, this means the lock will remain locked in a power failure. Fail-secure mechanisms prioritize the security of the building, preventing unauthorized access during power outages.

This is particularly important for protecting sensitive areas, such as utility rooms, storage areas, and other critical infrastructure within the building.

**Pros:**

1. **Enhanced Security:** Prevents unauthorized access during power failures, maintaining the security of the building and its occupants.

2. **Protection of Critical Areas:** Ensures that sensitive areas remain secured, safeguarding critical infrastructure and valuable assets.

3. **Reduced Vulnerability:** Less susceptible to tampering, as cutting power does not compromise the security of the locks.

**Cons:**

1. **Safety Risk:** Can pose a safety risk during emergencies if residents are unable to exit the building due to locked doors. This can be offset by having an override system (maybe one as simple as a key) so that staff can unlock doors in the event of an emergency.

2. **Non-Compliance with Fire Codes:** May not meet fire safety regulations requiring free egress during emergencies. This should be offset by consulting with experts and by incorporating contingencies in both the buildings EAP and Fire Safety Plan.

3. **Potential for Panic:** Residents might feel trapped and panicked if they cannot exit the building during a power failure. This can be offset through Training and Education.

### Balancing Safety and Security

The choice between fail-safe and fail-secure mechanisms is not straightforward and often requires a balanced approach tailored to the specific needs and layout of the building. Critical considerations include:

1. **Occupancy Safety:** Prioritizing the safety of residents and ensuring compliance with fire safety codes is **non-negotiable**. In areas where immediate access is necessary, such as main entry and exit points, fail-safe mechanisms are typically preferred, if not mandatory.

2. **Area Sensitivity:** For sensitive or high-security areas where unauthorized access must be strictly controlled, fail-secure mechanisms are appropriate. These areas can include data centers, utility rooms, and storage areas for valuable equipment.

3. **Redundancy and Backup Power:** Implementing backup power solutions, such as uninterruptible power supplies (UPS) or generators, can mitigate the risks associated with power failures. This ensures that security systems remain operational and can function according to their design (fail-safe or fail-secure) even during power outages.

4. **Hybrid Solutions:** In some cases, a hybrid approach might be the best solution. For example, main exit doors might be equipped with fail-safe locks, while sensitive, internal areas use fail-secure mechanisms. This ensures both safety and security are addressed appropriately.

## Conclusion and Key Takeaways

Effective access control is a cornerstone of residential security, integrating technological, procedural, and educational measures to safeguard buildings such as condominiums and their residents. Access control systems must be designed not only to facilitate authorized entry but also to deter and detect unauthorized attempts. A comprehensive approach, combining physical infrastructure, technological solutions, and community engagement, is essential to achieving this balance.

Key takeaways from this chapter include:

1. **Access Control Basics**: Effective access control relies on three key elements—something you have (e.g., key, fob), something you know (e.g., access code), and something you are (e.g., biometric data). Stricter facilities benefit from layered approaches using multiple elements.

2. **Procedures and Training**: Access control measures are only as strong as the people implementing them. Regular staff training and resident education are critical for identifying vulnerabilities and fostering a security-conscious culture.

3. **Key Management**: The proper handling, storage, and monitoring of master and unit keys are non-negotiable. Layers of security, such as locked key cabinets and video surveillance, help mitigate risks.

4. **Tailgating and Lockbox Security**: These are common vulnerabilities in residential buildings. Tailgating can be addressed through resident awareness and reporting, while lockboxes must be monitored and secured to prevent exploitation by intruders.

5. **Technological Integration**: Modern systems like electronic fobs, biometric systems, and intercoms enhance security but must be properly configured and maintained. Changing default settings and ensuring unique configurations are vital to avoid common mistakes.

6. **Fail-Safe vs. Fail-Secure**: Choosing between these mechanisms depends on balancing safety (fail-safe) and security (fail-secure). Tailored approaches, often incorporating backup power and hybrid solutions, ensure that both needs are met effectively.

7. **Resident Empowerment and Awareness**: Engaging residents as active participants in building security strengthens overall protection. Regular communication, education, and feedback loops create a culture of shared responsibility.

8. **Emergency Preparedness:** Incorporating access control decisions into the Emergency Action Plan (EAP) ensures that systems are robust and functional during crises, while compliance with fire safety regulations prioritizes resident safety.

By adopting a multifaceted approach to access control, residential buildings can address architectural, operational, and human factors that influence security. A well-implemented access control strategy not only protects the residents and their property but also builds trust and fosters a sense of safety within the community.

# CHAPTER 4

## *Security Lighting*

**Overview**

Lighting is a critical tool used to deter and detect potential intruders to the property. Efficient lighting must also be integrated with appropriate Video Surveillance Systems to ensure that images of unwanted activities are captured in a manner that will support proper identification and prosecution if warranted. An example of this not being done correctly is in the title picture for this chapter – one must look very closely to see that there is a camera in the area.

Security lighting serves multiple purposes:

- **Deterrence:** Well-lit areas discourage potential intruders and vandals.

- **Visibility:** Enhances the ability of security personnel and residents to observe activities in and around the condominium.

- **Identification:** Crucial for recognizing and documenting details such as vehicle colors, license plates, and other distinguishing features.

Lighting levels may be measured in Lux or Foot Candles. The table below is an example of accepted security lighting in Foot Candles (fc) and will be used as a reference to the measured light levels.

| Area | Recommended Lighting Levels |
|---|---|
| Walkways | 1.0 – 4.0 fc |
| Roadways | 0.5 - 2.0 fc |
| Entrances | 10.0 fc |
| Open Yards | 2.0 fc |
| Parking Garage | 5.0 fc to a horizontal ratio of 4:1 |

To evaluate the security effectiveness of lighting for the building. light meter readings should be taken at various locations around the property. These locations may include garage entrances, pedestrian entrances, receiving doors, courtyard, and other high traffic common elements.

**Boundary Lighting**

Perimeter security lighting is most effective when it is properly focused on the boundary or property line of the facility, as per the discussion in the Perimeter Protection chapter. This strategic placement of lighting helps in creating a secure perimeter, deterring potential intruders before they even approach the building. Accepted security standard guidelines indicate that lighting should be directed toward these critical boundary areas.

When upgrading or installing new lighting, it is essential to ensure that these lights are bright enough to illuminate the entire boundary clearly. This approach not only discourages unauthorized entry, but also assists in the identification and capture of individuals engaging in suspicious activities near the perimeter.

**Occupancy Lighting**

Occupancy sensors have emerged as a highly effective tool for improving security and energy efficiency in condominiums and residential buildings. These sensors, when integrated with strategic lighting systems, offer significant advantages that go beyond mere illumination. By ensuring that lights are activated ONLY when needed, occupancy sensors not only contribute to energy conservation but also act as a potent deterrent against potential intrusions.

*Energy Conservation: A Sustainable Approach*

One of the primary benefits of occupancy sensors is their ability to optimize energy usage. Traditional lighting systems often operate on fixed schedules or remain illuminated continuously, leading to unnecessary energy consumption. In contrast, occupancy sensors activate lights only when movement is detected, significantly reducing electricity usage in areas such as hallways, stairwells, parking garages, and utility rooms.

For instance, in stairwells or common areas of residential buildings, occupancy sensors ensure that some (not all) lights are off when the space is unoccupied. This functionality is particularly beneficial in reducing the carbon footprint of buildings, aligning with the growing emphasis on sustainability in urban planning. Additionally, these energy savings translate into cost reductions, which can benefit both property managers and residents by lowering utility expenses.

### Enhancing Security Through Sudden Illumination

Occupancy sensors also play a crucial role in enhancing building security. When these sensors detect motion, they trigger lightning in the area, which can be an effective psychological deterrent for potential intruders. The sudden illumination not only disrupts the intruder's activities but also increases their chances of being noticed, causing them to reconsider their intentions.

The deterrence factor is particularly effective in areas that are typically unoccupied, such as stairwells, parking garages, or secluded corners of a property. For instance, an intruder attempting to access a poorly lit stairwell may be startled by the sudden activation of lights. The intruder, thinking they have been noticed, may decide to flee. This proactive measure serves as a non-confrontational method to enhance the safety of residents and reduce incidents of unauthorized access or vandalism.

### Integration with Surveillance Systems

When paired with a surveillance system, occupancy sensors become even more impactful. Modern buildings with robust security plans often rely on a combination of physical presence, technology, and procedural measures. Occupancy sensors, when integrated with security cameras, provide an added layer of intelligence to the surveillance setup.

For example, if lights in a stairwell are triggered by motion, a camera covering that area can be programmed to send an alert to the security control room or concierge desk. Guards monitoring the system can then assess the situation in real time, distinguishing between residents, delivery personnel, or potential intruders. This immediate feedback enables security personnel to respond appropriately, reducing the likelihood of false alarms and ensuring swift intervention when needed.

Additionally, this integration enhances situational awareness. Guards are not just passively observing; they are equipped with actionable information, enabling them to focus their attention on specific areas of concern. In larger residential complexes, this can be a game-changer, as it maximizes the efficiency of the security team while minimizing blind spots.

### Strategic Placement for Maximum Effectiveness

The effectiveness of occupancy lighting systems depends heavily on their strategic placement within the building. Areas with high security risks or frequent but intermittent usage are prime candidates for sensor installation. Key locations include:

- Stairwells: Often secluded and less frequently used, stairwells benefit greatly from occupancy lighting. Sudden illumination in these areas can deter loitering and unauthorized access.

- Parking Garages: Vast and dimly lit parking areas can be intimidating for residents and a target for criminal activity. Motion-activated lights enhance visibility, making these spaces safer.

- Utility Rooms: Spaces such as electrical closets or storage rooms are often overlooked but can be targets for tampering. Sensors ensure these areas are monitored without requiring constant lighting.

- Perimeter Pathways: Outdoor pathways around the building can be fitted with motion-activated lighting to enhance security and resident safety during nighttime hours.

Proper placement not only improves the utility of the sensors but also ensures that they contribute effectively to both energy efficiency and security.

### Addressing Resident Concerns

While the benefits of occupancy sensors are clear, it is essential to address potential concerns residents may have regarding their use. Privacy is a common concern, especially when sensors are integrated with cameras. To mitigate these concerns, transparency in the system's capabilities and usage is vital. Building management should clearly communicate how the sensors and camera function, including where they are placed (signage) and how the data is used and stored (security master plan).

Moreover, management should involve experts in the planning process, soliciting their feedback on the placement of sensors and addressing any reservations. This collaborative approach fosters trust and ensures the security measures are well-received by the community.

### Long-Term Benefits and Innovations

The adoption of occupancy lighting systems in residential buildings is not just a current trend but a step toward future-proofing properties. With advancements in smart home technologies, these systems are becoming increasingly sophisticated. Integration with smart building management systems allows for data collection and analysis, providing insights into patterns of use and potential vulnerabilities.

For instance, patterns of frequent activation in certain areas might indicate a need for additional security measures or reconfiguration of access points. Similarly, data on low usage can help optimize energy consumption further by fine-tuning the sensitivity of the sensors.

Additionally, the integration of occupancy sensors with IoT (Internet of Things) devices opens possibilities for remote management and real-time updates. Property managers can monitor and adjust lighting systems through centralized platforms, making maintenance and optimization more efficient.

Occupancy sensors represent a valuable addition to the lighting and security infrastructure of condominium and residential buildings. Their dual benefits of energy conservation and enhanced security make them a practical choice for property managers and residents alike. By providing a sustainable solution to energy use while acting as a proactive deterrent against intruders, these systems contribute to safer, more efficient living environments. When strategically implemented and integrated with surveillance technologies, occupancy lighting transforms from a convenience into a cornerstone of modern residential security.

**Areas of Focus for Security Lighting**

**Walkways**

Walkways require consistent lighting levels ranging from 1.0 to 4.0 fc. Proper illumination of walkways ensures safe passage for residents and deters potential intruders. Light meter readings should be periodically taken to ensure that these areas maintain the required lighting levels. Inadequate lighting in walkways can lead to safety and trip hazards and reduce the overall safety and security of the property.

**Roadways**

Roadways within the property should have lighting levels between 0.5 to 2.0 fc. Adequate lighting on roadways enhances visibility for drivers and pedestrians, reducing the risk of accidents and making it more difficult for intruders to approach unnoticed. The lighting in these areas should also be sufficient lighting to ensure that vehicles, specifically license plates, are easily identified both visually and by any camera system.

**Entrances**

Entrances are critical points of security and require higher lighting levels, specifically around 10.0 fc. Brightly lit entrances make it easier for surveillance cameras to capture clear images of individuals entering and leaving the premises (a natural chokepoint). This level of illumination also provides a welcoming and secure environment for residents and visitors. In addition, our reports usually recommend that the civic address for each building by well lite – property maintenance theory from CPTED (pride in care of property).

## Open Yards

Open yards should be illuminated with lighting levels around 2.0 fc. Proper lighting in these areas helps deter unauthorized activities and ensures that surveillance systems can effectively monitor large, open spaces. In addition, as highlighted under the CPTED section, trees and landscaping should be trimmed to ensure that they do not interfere with the transmission of light.

## Parking Garages

Parking garages present unique security challenges and require lighting levels of 5.0 fc with a horizontal ratio of 4:1. This specific lighting ratio ensures that all areas of the parking garage are well lit, reducing shadows and dark corners where intruders could hide. This is the area where a lot of high rise & condominium residents feel some discomfort when traveling. Enhanced lighting levels will help alleviate these fears at ease. Regular light meter inspections in these areas will help maintain the appropriate lighting levels, enhance the resident comfort in their building and ensure safety and security for all users.

## Addressing Problem Areas

### Stairwells

Exterior stairwells have traditionally been a magnet to attract bad behavior. Reports of intrusion in these areas highlight the critical need for adequate lighting (+patrols +camera systems). These areas are often very dark – we have had some not even register any lighting levels (0.00 fc) on a meter. As these areas are traditionally out of public sight (Natural Surveillance), bad actors will migrate to these areas for illegal activity. Two such examples that are commonly reported in exterior stairwells (usually leading in and out of a garage or other exterior building) are prostitution and drug use.

To mitigate these issues, it is essential to increase the lighting levels in stairwells. Additionally, installing occupancy sensors in stairwells can provide an immediate response to movement, serving the dual purpose of both alerting security personnel to any activity in these areas, as well as acting as a security deterrent. These areas, in addition to being protected by lighting, should also be regularly patrolled and (when possible) monitored by cameras.

## Courtyard and Receiving Doors

Light meter readings should also be conducted around the courtyard and receiving doors. These areas can be vulnerable points for unauthorized access if not properly illuminated. Ensuring that these locations have adequate lighting can help deter intruders and facilitate the capture of clear surveillance images.

## Integrating Lighting with Surveillance Systems

Efficient security lighting must be seamlessly integrated with video surveillance systems. Properly illuminated areas enable surveillance cameras to capture high-quality images that are essential for identifying and prosecuting intruders. This integration is crucial for creating a comprehensive security system that maximizes both deterrence and detection.

### *Lighting Conditions and Colour Identification*

Proper lighting conditions are essential for accurate colour identification. Different types of lighting can significantly affect the perception of colours:

- **Natural Light:** Provides the most accurate colour representation. However, this lighting has its limitations, most notably its usefulness in daytime hours and exterior areas only.

- **Fluorescent Lighting:** Commonly used in parking garages and outdoor areas. Fluorescent lights can sometimes distort colours, making it challenging to identify vehicle colours accurately.

- **LED Lighting:** Increasingly popular due to its energy efficiency and longevity. LED lights offer a more accurate colour rendering compared to fluorescent lights, making them ideal for security purposes.

- **High-Intensity Discharge (HID) Lighting:** Often used in large outdoor areas. HID lights provide bright illumination, but can alter the appearance of colours, potentially complicating identification.

## Choosing the Right Lighting Fixtures

Selecting the appropriate lighting fixtures is vital for achieving optimal security lighting. Fixtures should be durable, weather-resistant, and provide consistent illumination. As noted above, LED lights are often recommended due to their energy efficiency, longevity, and bright, clear light output.

### *Best Practices for Security Lighting*

To ensure optimal security lighting for accurate vehicle and object identification, consider the following best practices:

1. **Use LED Lighting:** LEDs provide superior colour rendering, ensuring that vehicle colours and other details are accurately represented. They also have a longer lifespan and are energy efficient.

2. **Ensure Uniform Lighting:** Avoid areas of excessive brightness or deep shadows. Uniform lighting reduces the risk of distorted colour perception and improves overall visibility.

3. **Regular Maintenance:** Conduct routine checks and maintenance to ensure all lights are functioning correctly. Replace any burnt-out or flickering lights promptly.

4. **Positioning and Angling:** Proper positioning and angling of lights can minimize glare and shadows, enhancing the ability to identify colours and details.

5. **Use Colour Temperature Appropriately:** Opt for lighting with a colour temperature that closely resembles natural daylight. A colour temperature of around 5000K is ideal for accurate colour identification.

6. **Integration with Security Cameras:** Ensure that lighting works in tandem with security cameras. Properly lit areas enhance camera footage quality, making it easier to identify vehicles and objects.

## Conclusion and Takeaways

Effective security includes well-designed lighting that deters unauthorized access, enhances visibility, and supports identification efforts. Each area of a property has specific lighting requirements that must be customized to ensure both security and usability. Integrating lighting with surveillance systems and other security measures creates a cohesive and robust defense against potential intrusions, forming the foundation of a holistic security design. Leveraging modern lighting solutions, such as LED fixtures and occupancy sensors, further optimizes security while improving energy efficiency. Routine evaluations and updates to the lighting system are essential to address evolving security challenges and maintain long-term effectiveness.

1. **Lighting as a Security Tool:** Lighting serves as a crucial component of security, fulfilling roles of deterrence, visibility, and identification while supporting surveillance systems.

2. **Measuring and Maintaining Lighting Levels:** Proper lighting levels, measured in Foot Candles (fc), are essential across various

areas like walkways, roadways, entrances, and parking garages to ensure safety, comfort, and security.

3. **Boundary and Occupancy Lighting**: Strategically placed boundary lighting deters intrusions before reaching the property, while occupancy sensors conserve energy and enhance security by detecting movement.

4. **Addressing Problem Areas**: Stairwells, courtyards, and receiving doors are vulnerable spots that require enhanced lighting, regular patrols, and camera monitoring to mitigate risks.

5. **Integration with Surveillance Systems**: Properly illuminated areas enable high-quality surveillance footage, essential for identifying and prosecuting unauthorized activities.

6. **Lighting Conditions and Colour Identification**: Different lighting types affect colour perception, with LED lighting emerging as the most reliable option for accurate identification and energy efficiency.

7. **Best Practices for Security Lighting**: Uniform lighting, regular maintenance, proper fixture selection, and integration with security cameras are critical for achieving effective security.

By focusing on these principles, properties can significantly enhance their security posture, providing a safer environment for residents and visitors.

# CHAPTER 5

## *Video Surveillance Systems*

In recent years, the technology available to condominiums has improved significantly and has become far more affordable. Years ago, the Video Surveillance System (VSS - previously referred to as the CCTV system) consisted of a laborious process with changing VHS tapes in the recorder daily and the continual over-writing of tapes (which wore out). In addition, camera locations were occasionally chosen based on the considerable expense of running cables through the building to carry the signals back to the recorder. Recent technical advances in the equipment have made security VSS implementations far more useful to residential buildings such as condominiums in several different ways.

## Advances in Video Surveillance Technology

The introduction of new technologies, such as the NVR (network video recorder), has significantly reduced setup costs and the need for extensive cabling. Some modern NVR systems only require a power source and an internet signal for each camera, simplifying the installation process and increasing flexibility in camera placement. Furthermore, technological advances have introduced solar-powered security cameras with SIM cards that eliminate the need for either a power source or cables. These cameras are well suited for townhome condominiums with limited common elements to house DVRS and monitors.

Storage technology has also seen substantial improvements, with costs for storage medium decreasing and capacity increasing. This allows buildings to store video footage for extended periods — months, years, or even indefinitely, depending on their specific needs and regulations. In addition, as this storage is done online (for the most part) it eliminates the need for a physical location for storage mediums (like USB and external drives) and decreases the likelihood of missing information (lost or damaged VHS tapes).

However, despite these advances, some condominiums remain hesitant to invest in new VSS technology due to fears of rapid obsolescence. While it is true that technology continues to evolve, it's important to understand that obsolete does not equate to ineffectiveness. An older system can still be effective if it was properly designed to meet the buildings' security requirements. Thus, VSS should be designed or redesigned with growth and expansion in mind, ensuring longevity and adaptability.

**Back-Up Power and Storage Best Practices**

A reliable VSS should have a backup power source to ensure continuous operation during power outages. This can include Uninterruptible Power Supplies (UPS) for each camera and recorder, as well as generators for more extended outages. Backup power ensures that critical surveillance footage is captured even during emergencies, which is essential for both security and liability purposes. This is very important because there are intruders that will seek to take advantage of power outages (RE Looting), as VSS and Access Control systems may be subject to disruption.

When it comes to storage, best practices recommend using back-up systems to prevent data loss. This might include on-site storage combined with cloud backups. Regularly scheduled maintenance checks and data integrity tests are also crucial to ensure that stored footage remains accessible and uncorrupted.

As for how long a building should archive video footage, it generally depends on local regulations and the specific needs of the building. A common recommendation is to retain footage for a *minimum* of 30 days, but in some cases, longer retention periods may be necessary. For instance, if a condominium has frequent incidents or legal requirements, a retention period of 90 days or more might be appropriate.

**Developing a Security Camera Policy**

Having a clear and comprehensive security camera policy is essential for the effective and ethical use of video surveillance systems. This policy should detail under what circumstances, and by whom, footage can be accessed and reviewed. Typically, access should be restricted to authorized personnel like the property manager, head of security, or designated board members. It is not recommended that cameras be used for investigating rule violations.

The policy should outline procedures for requesting and approving access to footage, ensuring that all requests are documented and justified. It should also specify how and when footage can be shared with law enforcement or other external parties, always adhering to privacy laws and regulations.

Sharing security footage directly with owners or residents, no matter how well-intentioned, can lead to significant privacy and legal concerns. Allowing unrestricted access risks breaching confidentiality agreements, violating privacy laws, and exposing the building management to potential liability. By delivering footage exclusively to law enforcement and only upon their formal request, condominium boards and property managers ensure that evidence is handled appropriately, safeguarding the integrity of investigations and protecting the privacy of all residents. This policy also reinforces trust within the community, demonstrating a commitment to fair and professional handling of sensitive information.

## Ethical Use of Security Cameras

It's important to emphasize that security cameras should NOT be used to monitor staff performance. This practice may lead to creating a hostile work environment and may violate employment contracts. Monitoring staff performance using security cameras without proper justification and notification could lead to legal repercussions and unmotivated staff. Therefore, VSS should be utilized strictly for the security purposes for which they were intended, such as preventing unauthorized access, vandalism, and monitoring criminal activities.

## Date and Time Stamps

Many times, during security audits, cameras have been found with inconsistent or incorrect dates and times. Ensuring the accuracy of the date and time stamp on your camera system is paramount for maintaining the integrity and reliability of your security infrastructure. In the event of a security incident, accurate timestamps provide crucial evidence that can be relied upon during investigations and legal proceedings. An incorrect date or timestamp can cast doubt on the validity of the entire camera system, potentially undermining the entire case and rendering the evidence inadmissible. Therefore, regular checks and adjustments to the system's date and time settings are essential. By doing so, management can safeguard against discrepancies that could compromise the credibility of the surveillance data, ensuring that the system serves its intended purpose effectively and trustworthily. As part of an annual activity, managers should check the cameras system after each daylight savings change.

## Warnings About Dummy and Hidden Cameras

The use of dummy or fake cameras can create a false sense of security. While they *may* deter some potential wrongdoers, they do not provide any real security benefit and can leave a residential building or condominium vulnerable to more determined criminals. Previously, fake cameras were popular because they were cheap. As in most things, cheaper is not necessarily better and, in these cases, it is the strong opinion of this book that the risk incurred by having a fake camera is much higher than the perceived savings. A Globe and Mail article highlighted the risks associated with dummy cameras, noting that they can give residents and staff a misleading impression of safety. **The risk associated with having a fake camera cannot be overstated enough.**

Hidden cameras also pose significant ethical and legal challenges. Recent news stories have shown that the use of hidden cameras can lead to severe privacy violations and legal consequences. It is crucial that all cameras are clearly visible and that their presence is communicated to residents and visitors through appropriate signage. Transparency in surveillance practices helps maintain trust and ensures compliance with privacy laws.

## Prioritizing Camera Placement and Ratings

When evaluating or upgrading a VSS, a starting point could be to prioritize camera placements based on their importance to the security system and their ability to provide accurate information. Cameras should be rated on a scale from 1 to 3, where:

- **Priority 1: Critical to Security System**

- **Priority 2: Necessary Security System**

- **Priority 3: Ideal to Security System**

And their effectiveness should be assessed as follows:

- **Rating 1: Exceeds Security Requirements**

- **Rating 2: Meets Security Requirements**

- **Rating 3: Below Security Requirements**

Critical cameras (Priority 1) should be placed at key entry and exit points, high-traffic areas, and other vulnerable spots. These cameras should exceed security requirements to ensure the highest level of resolution and protection. Necessary cameras (Priority 2) should cover additionally important areas, meeting all security standards. These cameras are usually popular in elevators, stairwells, and other common elements like function and party rooms. Ideal cameras (Priority 3) can enhance overall coverage but are not essential.

## Exterior Cameras

In today's security landscape, exterior cameras that monitor the approach to a building's entrances are rapidly becoming an asset. These cameras offer multiple layers of security and provide significant advantages in both deterring and responding to potential security threats.

### Deter Unwanted Behavior

One of the primary advantages of exterior cameras is their deterrent effect. Intruders, vandals, and other potential wrongdoers are often discouraged by the presence of visible surveillance equipment (Perimeter Protection). Knowing they are being watched, these individuals are more inclined to conduct illegal activities in an area that is less monitored. This deterrent effect extends not only to the immediate vicinity of the building, but also to the broader neighborhood, creating a safer community for residents and visitors alike.

*Capturing Pre-Entry Activities*

Intruders are typically more vigilant about avoiding cameras once inside a building, using clothing such as hoodies and masks. However, exterior cameras may be able to capture activities and behaviors before the intruders can conceal their identities or intentions. By monitoring the approach to the building, these cameras can document suspicious behavior or actions that indicate a potential threat. This early detection can play an important part in pre-emptively addressing security breaches. In addition, if the cameras are monitored in real time, these cameras are useful in providing proactive information.

For example, individuals who linger around entrances (potentially seeking to follow or tailgate into the building), or who exhibit unusual behavior, can be identified and monitored, allowing security personnel to respond promptly. This proactive surveillance significantly enhances the overall security posture of the condominium.

*Vehicle Identification*

Exterior cameras are especially valuable for monitoring vehicles approaching the building. In many cases, intruders may use a vehicle to access the premises. By capturing detailed footage of vehicles, including make, model, color, and most importantly, the license plate number, these cameras provide critical information that can be used in investigations.

*Legal and Insurance Benefits*

The presence of exterior cameras also has legal and insurance advantages. In case of a dispute or claim, video footage serves as compelling evidence to resolve conflicts or support claims. For instance, in incidents of property damage or personal injury (such as a slip and fall) near the building, the recorded footage can provide clear documentation of events as they unfolded, aiding in legal proceedings or insurance claims. In addition, from management's perspective, the camera may capture mitigating actions on the part of management (such as regular salting /sanding of snow-covered entrances).

Video camera systems are undeniably a critical component of any security infrastructure, providing invaluable evidence and real-time monitoring capabilities. However, their effectiveness as a deterrent has diminished in recent years, particularly since the pandemic, as masks and other face coverings have become commonplace, making identification more challenging. Moreover, some intruders are now much more brazen, disregarding the presence of cameras altogether. This shift underscores the necessity of integrating cameras into a comprehensive security strategy that includes patrols and other proactive measures. Combining technology with human vigilance creates a layered approach that can effectively deter, detect, and respond to potential threats, ensuring a more robust security posture.

## Advantages and Disadvantages of AI Cameras

AI cameras have emerged as a transformative technology in the field of building and residential security. These cameras leverage advanced machine learning algorithms to identify patterns, detect anomalies, and respond to potential threats in real-time. While they offer numerous advantages, they are not a standalone solution. This section will explore the strengths and limitations of AI cameras, emphasizing the importance of integrating them with a comprehensive security strategy, including a dedicated security response team.

### *Advantages of AI Cameras*

*Real-Time Threat Detection:* AI cameras can analyze footage in real-time to detect suspicious activities, such as unauthorized entry, loitering, or the presence of weapons. This capability significantly reduces the reaction time for addressing potential security threats.

*Proactive Monitoring:* Unlike traditional surveillance systems that require manual monitoring, AI cameras can proactively identify and alert security personnel to unusual activities, reducing the risk of human error.

*Enhanced Accuracy:* Through continuous learning, AI cameras can improve their ability to differentiate between genuine threats and false alarms, such as distinguishing between a person and an animal.

*Integration with Other Technologies:* AI cameras can seamlessly integrate with access control systems, alarm systems, and mobile applications, creating a unified security ecosystem.

*Cost Efficiency:* By automating monitoring tasks and reducing the need for constant human oversight, AI cameras can lower long-term operational costs.

*Data Collection and Analysis:* AI cameras collect vast amounts of data, which can be analyzed to identify trends, improve security protocols, and enhance overall safety strategies.

## Disadvantages of AI Cameras

*High Initial Investment:* AI cameras and their associated infrastructure often require a significant upfront investment, which can be a barrier for smaller residential properties.

*Dependence on Technology:* These systems are dependent on consistent power and network connectivity. A failure in either can render the cameras ineffective.

*Privacy Concerns:* The advanced monitoring capabilities of AI cameras can raise privacy issues among residents, particularly if the scope of surveillance is not clearly communicated and managed.

*False Positives and Negatives:* While AI improves accuracy over time, there is still a risk of false alarms or failure to detect genuine threats, especially in complex or crowded environments.

*Maintenance and Updates:* Regular updates and maintenance are essential to ensure the cameras remain effective. This can add to the operational costs and complexity.

*Limited Contextual Understanding:* AI cameras can identify anomalies but may lack the contextual understanding that human operators possess. For instance, a person lingering in a lobby might be a resident waiting for a ride, not a security threat.

## *The Need for a Security Response Team*

AI cameras are powerful tools, but their effectiveness hinges on the presence of a well-trained security response team. Cameras can detect and alert, but they cannot intervene in real-time incidents, de-escalate conflicts, or provide a human presence that deters criminal activity.

A dedicated security team ensures that:

- Alerts from AI cameras are promptly investigated.

- Incidents are managed professionally and safely.

- Residents feel reassured by the visible presence of security personnel.

While AI cameras represent a significant leap forward in security technology, they are **not silver bullets**. Their implementation should be part of a layered security approach that combines technology, trained personnel, and robust policies. By integrating AI cameras with a responsive and proactive security team, residential buildings can achieve a higher level of safety and security while addressing the limitations of relying solely on technology.

## Takeaways and Conclusions

The advancements in VSS technology present an unparalleled opportunity for residential buildings like condominiums to strengthen their security frameworks effectively and affordably. However, successful implementation depends on adopting a strategic approach—prioritizing ethical practices, regular maintenance, comprehensive policies, and the integration of reliable backup systems. By embracing these advancements thoughtfully, condominium managers can significantly enhance the safety and trust of their communities.

1. **Technological Advancements Enhance Usability and Affordability**

Modern video surveillance systems (VSS) like NVRs have simplified installation and reduced costs, making them accessible to more condominiums. The availability of solar-powered cameras and cloud storage further streamlines implementation, making them suitable for diverse residential setups.

## 2. Importance of Future-Proofing Security Systems

Although some condominiums hesitate to adopt new technologies due to concerns about obsolescence, systems designed with scalability and adaptability can remain effective and relevant over time.

## 3. Critical Role of Backup Systems

Ensuring uninterrupted VSS operation during power outages through backup power systems, such as UPS units and generators, is essential. Regular maintenance and dual on-site and cloud-based backups mitigate risks of data loss.

## 4. Retention and Compliance with Regulations

Storage duration should align with local regulations and the specific needs of the condominium. While 30 days is a standard retention period, high-risk properties may require longer durations.

## 5. Establishing Comprehensive Policies

A robust security camera policy is vital for ethical, effective VSS use. It should define access protocols, restrict footage review to authorized personnel, and comply with privacy laws, ensuring transparency and trust among residents.

## 6. Ethical Considerations in Camera Use

Cameras should not monitor staff performance or be used for rule enforcement. Ethical surveillance builds trust and avoids legal and morale issues.

7. **Accurate Date and Time Stamps are Non-Negotiable**

   Timestamps ensure the reliability and credibility of video footage in legal and investigative contexts. Regular checks, especially during daylight savings time changes, are crucial.

8. **Avoiding Dummy and Hidden Cameras**

   Fake cameras provide no actual security benefits and may create a false sense of safety. Hidden cameras pose significant ethical and legal challenges. Visible, well-communicated surveillance is always preferable.

9. **Prioritizing Camera Placement for Maximum Effectiveness**

   Cameras should be rated and placed based on their criticality and ability to meet security requirements. Entry points, high-traffic areas, and vulnerable zones are top priorities.

10. **Advantages of Exterior Cameras**

    Exterior cameras enhance security by deterring unwanted behavior, capturing pre-entry activities, and identifying vehicles, including license plates. They also provide valuable evidence for legal and insurance purposes.

11. **Building a Proactive Security Posture**

    Real-time monitoring of exterior cameras allows for early detection and intervention, enabling security personnel to respond to potential threats before incidents escalate.

# CHAPTER 6

# *Crime Prevention through Environmental Design (CPTED)*

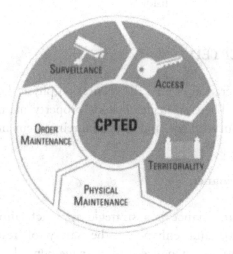

## Introduction

Crime Prevention through Environmental Design (CPTED) is a multidisciplinary approach to deterring criminal behavior through environmental design. In the context of condominium and high-rise security in Canada, CPTED principles can play a crucial role in enhancing safety, reducing crime, and fostering a sense of community among residents. This chapter explores both the foundational (1st Generation) and advanced (2nd Generation) principles of CPTED, providing practical applications for building and condominium settings. We will then introduce 3rd generation CPTED, which should be of interest for developers and builders.

## 1st Generation CPTED

The first generation of CPTED focuses on physical design strategies to reduce crime. These strategies include property maintenance, access control, natural surveillance, and territorial reinforcement.

## Property Maintenance

Property Maintenance is a strategic approach aimed at reducing criminal behavior and enhancing the safety of residents through effective property maintenance and management. In the context of high-rise buildings, CPTED principles focus on maintaining a well-kept environment to deter crime and promote a sense of security. This concept of CPTED is grounded in the broken window theory. This theory posits that visible signs of disorder and neglect, such as broken windows, graffiti, and litter, create an environment that encourages further vandalism and criminal behavior. By maintaining properties in good condition, addressing repairs promptly, and ensuring that public spaces are clean and well-kept, a sense of order and respect is fostered. This proactive approach not only deters potential offenders by signaling that the area is monitored and cared for but also promotes a feeling of safety and community pride among residents. Effective property maintenance, therefore, is a critical element of CPTED strategies, reinforcing the overall security and quality of the living environment. For instance, promptly replacing any burnt-out lights in common areas such as parking lots, hallways, and entrances ensures that these spaces are well-lit, reducing opportunities for criminal activities to occur under the cover of darkness. Additionally, addressing vandalism swiftly not only restores the aesthetic appeal of the property but also sends a clear message that the community is vigilant and proactive in maintaining a safe environment. Neglecting these aspects can lead to an increase in criminal activities, as poorly maintained properties often attract undesirable behavior. Studies have shown that in the absence of action on the part of the building, these security incidents will increase in both severity and frequency. By integrating CPTED Property Maintenance strategies, property managers can create a safer and more secure living environment for all residents.

## Access Control

Access control was covered in a previous chapter. It is designed to restrict unauthorized entry to the building and its facilities. Effective measures include installing secure locks, controlled entry points, and electronic access systems such as key fobs or biometric scanners. Physical barriers like fences and gates also help manage access, ensuring that only authorized individuals can enter specific areas.

## Natural Surveillance

Another fundamental principle of CPTED is Natural Surveillance, which aims to maximize visibility and foster an environment where people can see and be seen. This concept is particularly relevant to high rise buildings, where the design and layout can significantly impact the residents' sense of security. Implementing Natural Surveillance in condominiums and other such buildings involves strategically placing windows, lighting, and common areas to ensure that there are minimal blind spots and that residents can observe their surroundings easily. For instance, employing the 7/2 rule – a guideline recommending that the lowest seven feet of a building should be kept clear of any obstructions (such as tree branches) while allowing visibility up to the first two floors—can enhance surveillance. This rule further proposes that shrubs and structures do not impede sightlines, making it difficult for potential intruders to hide and easier for residents to monitor activity. Simply put, tree branches should be cut up to a height of 7 feet, and bushes/shrubs should be trimmed down to a height of 2 feet. Other examples of natural surveillance include placing transparent barriers instead of opaque ones around entrance areas, ensuring that parking lots are well-lit and visible from multiple vantage points, and designing lobbies and common areas with ample windows facing the street. By incorporating these CPTED strategies, condominiums and other buildings can create safer, more vigilant communities.

## Territorial Reinforcement

Territorial Reinforcement, our last Gen1 principle of CPTED, plays a crucial role in enhancing the security of high-rise buildings such as condominiums. This concept involves using physical design elements to express ownership and establish clear boundaries between public, semi-public, and private spaces, thereby deterring potential criminal activities. One of the goals of Territorial Reinforcement is to create a level of discomfort in would-be intruders when they cross a barrier (either physical or phycological) to get to the interior of the property. Ideally, this discomfort may cause them to abandon their objective. In the context of multi-family buildings, effective territorial reinforcement can be achieved through strategic landscaping, the placement of fences, signage, and the design of communal areas. For instance, well-maintained gardens and distinct pathways lead to individual units' signals that the building owners are attentive and invested in their community, which can discourage intruders. By integrating these elements, condominiums can create an environment that not only enhances aesthetic appeal but also promotes safety and a sense of ownership among owners, tenants and residents.

Psychological barriers are an essential element of Territorial Reinforcement, leveraging subtle yet impactful cues to deter criminal activity. These barriers include symbolic markers such as custom welcome mats, nameplates, or unit-specific lighting, which create the impression that the space is closely monitored and personalized. When individuals encounter areas that exude a strong sense of belonging and order, they are less likely to feel anonymous, increasing the perceived risk of detection. Additionally, implementing controlled access points with visible security cameras and clear signage such as "Residents Only" or "Private Property" reinforces these psychological deterrents. The combination of physical and psychological boundaries fosters an environment where intruders are more likely to feel out of place and deterred, contributing to the overall security of the building.

## 2nd Generation CPTED: Social Factors

The second generation of CPTED incorporates social factors to complement the physical design strategies, aiming to enhance community cohesion and engagement. These factors are crucial in multifamily buildings such as condominiums and high-rise buildings, whose residents come from diverse backgrounds. In addition to creating a setting where a strong, cooperative community is fostered, it also can assist in resident satisfaction, leading to the reduction in complaints. This is an added benefit to the significant increase in the impact of the overall security of the building.

## Social Cohesion

Social cohesion refers to the strength of relationships and the sense of community among residents. Encouraging social interactions through community events, shared spaces, and resident committees can build trust and cooperation. A well-connected community is more likely to look out for each other and report suspicious activities, creating a collective sense of responsibility for safety. From the perspective of situational awareness, social cohesion is essentially the establishing of a baseline. When residents have an idea on who and what should be in the building, they are much more likely to note items that fall outside that "norm" and report them.

## Community Culture

Establishing a positive community culture involves promoting norms and values that prioritize safety and mutual respect. This can be achieved through resident handbooks, orientation sessions for new residents, and regular communication from the property management about safety practices and community standards. This is a reversing trend from previous years where management was very cautious about discussing security concerns as they were worried about causing scares, resident complaints, and dropping property values. It is the opinion of this book that open discussion on this subject will promote a sense of safety & security in the building. Contrastly, if it is perceived that the board or management is keeping information from the residents, specifically as it relates to security, this will amplify the fear and insecurity of the residents. The writer has been invited to several condominium AGMs to discuss safety and security topics. Using this forum as an education platform is an excellent opportunity to both demonstrate, and get resident buy-in, for the building's security policies. As of critical importance, many buildings have adopted a no-harassment policy to further cultivate this culture of respect in the condo and residential community.

## Incentives for Resident Participation

One of the more common questions is how buildings with limited budgets can implement a comprehensive security plan? A method to overcome this obstacle is by getting residents to buy into the building security policy. Creating platforms for resident participation in safety initiatives can enhance engagement. This might include recognizing and rewarding residents who actively contribute to safety programs, volunteering for neighborhood watch groups, or participating in community or town hall meetings. Incentives foster a proactive attitude toward maintaining a secure environment. This can be implemented through "see something, say something" signage that encourages residents to report security concerns for management action. As a caveat, it must be noted that if such a platform is put in place, it is incumbent on management to follow up on the reported security concerns. Failure to do so will sow dissent amount the residents and can lead to feelings of neglect. The best case is that they will stop reporting security concerns as they will be perceived as a waste of time and effort.

## Building Trust with Security Personnel

Developing a positive relationship between residents and security personnel is vital. Security staff should be approachable, well-trained, and integrated into the community. As part of the training, security and concierge should be trained to be an impartial third-party contractor within the building. Part of this is **not** getting involved in personal issues or commenting on management decisions, unless it is to support it. This will prevent the erosion of trust in the security team on the part of management. In addition, when guards participate in the "politics" of the building, it reflects poorly on them and the company.

Regular interaction and transparency about security measures can build trust and ensure residents feel comfortable reporting issues and cooperating with security efforts Integrating both 1st and 2nd Generation CPTED principles can create a holistic approach to condominium security. Here are practical applications:

1. **Conduct Regular Security Audits**: Regular security audits can identify vulnerabilities and assess the effectiveness of current security measures. These audits should consider both physical and social aspects of security, providing a comprehensive strategy to enhance safety

2. **Enhance Landscaping and Lighting**: Maintain landscaping to eliminate potential hiding spots and ensure pathways and common areas are well-lit. Proper lighting not only deters criminals but also makes residents feel safer when moving around the property at night.

3. **Install Advanced Access Control Systems**: Utilize electronic access systems to monitor and control entry points. Ensure these systems are regularly updated and maintained to prevent unauthorized access.

4. **Foster a Strong Community**: Organize regular social events, such as barbecues, holiday celebrations, and resident meetings, to build a sense of community. Encourage residents to get to know each other, which can enhance natural surveillance and collective vigilance.

5. **Engage Residents in Security Initiatives**: Create opportunities for residents to participate in safety programs and provide feedback on security measures. This involvement can increase their commitment to maintaining a secure environment.

6. **Promote Communication and Education**: Keep residents informed about security policies, recent incidents, and preventive measures through newsletters, emails, and bulletin boards. Educate them on the importance of security and their role in maintaining it.

## Introducing Third Generation CPTED

Crime Prevention Through Environmental Design (CPTED) has evolved significantly since its inception, adapting to the challenges of modern urban living. With residential high-rise buildings becoming a cornerstone of urban development, the application of Third Generation CPTED principles offers an opportunity to create safer, more inclusive, and resilient communities.

## Introducing Third Generation CPTED

CPTED has traditionally focused on environmental modifications to deter crime (First Generation) and fostering social cohesion (Second Generation). The Third Generation builds upon these foundations by integrating broader concepts of sustainability, resilience, and community well-being. It emphasizes a proactive approach to safety that considers the complex interplay of physical, social, and digital spaces within residential high-rises.

## Physical Design with Resilience in Mind

The physical design of residential high-rises is a critical component of Third Generation CPTED. This involves:

- **Natural Surveillance:** Incorporating open sightlines, well-lit common areas, and strategically placed windows to increase visibility. Balconies and terraces designed to overlook shared spaces can foster natural surveillance while enhancing community interaction.

- **Defensible Space:** Clear delineation between public, semi-private, and private areas reduce opportunities for unauthorized access. Features like gated lobbies, secure elevators, and keycard access systems can contribute to a layered security approach.

- **Sustainable Materials:** Using durable and vandal-resistant materials not only minimizes maintenance costs but also deters criminal activity. For instance, shatterproof glass and anti-graffiti coatings enhance both aesthetics and functionality.

## Social Cohesion and Community Building

High-rise buildings often face challenges in fostering a sense of community due to their vertical design and diverse demographics. Third Generation CPTED addresses this by:

- **Shared Spaces:** Designing multipurpose communal areas such as gyms, libraries, and rooftop gardens encourages social interaction and collaboration among residents.

- **Resident Engagement:** Organizing community events, workshops, and regular meetings helps build trust and mutual accountability. A strong community is inherently more resilient to crime.

- **Cultural Sensitivity:** Recognizing the diverse cultural backgrounds of residents and incorporating inclusive design elements ensures a sense of belonging for all.

## Integration of Technology

The digital aspect of Third Generation CPTED leverages technology to complement traditional strategies. Examples include:

- **Smart Surveillance:** Using AI-powered cameras and sensors to monitor high-risk areas while respecting privacy concerns. These systems can provide real-time alerts to security personnel.

- **Access Control Systems:** Implementing biometric entry systems and smartphone-based access reduces the risk of unauthorized entry.

- **Community Apps:** Developing platforms where residents can report maintenance issues, share updates, and communicate with building management fosters transparency and engagement.

## Sustainability and Environmental Stewardship

Sustainability is a hallmark of Third Generation CPTED. High-rises adopting these principles should aim to:

- **Energy Efficiency:** Utilize solar panels, energy-efficient lighting, and smart HVAC systems to reduce environmental impact while creating well-lit, safe environments.

- **Green Spaces:** Incorporating vegetation through vertical gardens, green roofs, and landscaped terraces not only enhances aesthetics but also reduces stress and promotes well-being.

- **Waste Management:** Implementing efficient recycling and waste disposal systems prevents the accumulation of debris, which can create opportunities for criminal activity.

## Resilience and Crisis Preparedness

Third Generation CPTED emphasizes readiness for emergencies, ensuring that high-rises can withstand both natural and man-made crises. Key strategies include:

- **Emergency Planning:** Establishing clear evacuation routes, emergency assembly areas, and regular fire and safety drills. This was covered in the first chapter of the book.

- **Community Resilience:** Training residents in first aid, self-defence, and basic disaster response empowers them to act decisively during crises.

- **Redundancy in Critical Systems:** Backup power supplies, water storage, and communication systems ensure functionality during extended outages.

## Challenges in Implementation

Despite its benefits, implementing Third Generation CPTED in high-rises is not without challenges:

1. **Cost Constraints:** Advanced technologies and sustainable materials often require significant upfront investment, which can deter developers and property managers.

2. **Resistance to Change:** Some stakeholders may resist adopting new security measures or community-building initiatives due to skepticism or inertia.

3. **Balancing Privacy and Security:** Integrating surveillance and access control systems must be done carefully to respect residents' privacy while ensuring safety.

4. **Diverse Demographics:** Addressing the varying needs and expectations of a multicultural and multigenerational resident base requires nuanced planning.

## The Path Forward: Recommendations for Stakeholders

### For Developers:

- Incorporate CPTED principles from the design phase to minimize retrofitting costs and ensure holistic integration.

- Engage with community members early to understand their concerns and priorities.

### For Property Managers:

- Regularly review and update security policies and technologies to stay ahead of emerging threats.

- Foster resident participation in decision-making processes to build trust and accountability.

**For Residents:**

- Participate in community events and training sessions to strengthen social ties and preparedness.

- Use provided platforms to report safety concerns and contribute to a proactive security culture.

Third Generation CPTED offers a transformative approach to safety and security in residential high-rises. By integrating physical design, social cohesion, technological innovation, sustainability, and resilience, it creates an environment where residents not only feel safe but also thrive. While challenges remain, the benefits of adopting these principles far outweigh the costs, paving the way for safer and more connected urban communities.

**Conclusion and Takeaways**

The integration of Crime Prevention Through Environmental Design (CPTED) principles in condominium and high-rise settings offers a robust framework for enhancing security, reducing crime, and fostering community well-being. This chapter highlighted the critical role of both 1st and 2nd Generation CPTED strategies in achieving these goals. While the physical design elements of 1st Generation CPTED, such as property maintenance, access control, natural surveillance, and territorial reinforcement, create a strong foundation for security, the social factors of 2nd Generation CPTED address the human element, enhancing trust, cohesion, and resident engagement.

By understanding and applying these principles, property managers, board members, and residents can collaboratively build safer and more inclusive communities. Each component—from maintaining a well-kept environment to fostering resident participation—contributes to a holistic approach to security that not only deters criminal behavior but also empowers residents to take an active role in safeguarding their living spaces.

**Takeaways**

1.  Property Maintenance is Essential: Maintaining a clean, well-kept environment signals vigilance and deters crime. Addressing repairs and vandalism promptly fosters a sense of security and community pride.

2.  Effective Access Control is Fundamental: Robust access control measures, such as secure locks, key fobs, and biometric systems, ensure that only authorized individuals can access the property, reducing the risk of unauthorized entry.

3.  Natural Surveillance Enhances Visibility: Strategic placement of lighting, windows, and landscaping reduces blind spots and makes it easier for residents to observe their surroundings, increasing safety and vigilance.

4.  Territorial Reinforcement Deters Intruders: Clear boundaries, both physical and psychological, establish ownership and discourage unauthorized access. Elements like signage, landscaping, and symbolic markers create a secure and welcoming atmosphere.

5.  Social Factors Amplify Security Measures: Building social cohesion, fostering community culture, and encouraging resident participation strengthen the collective responsibility for safety and create a more engaged community.

6.  Trust with Security Personnel is Vital: Security staff should be approachable and impartial, integrating seamlessly into the community while maintaining professionalism to build trust and encourage resident cooperation.

7. Comprehensive Security Audits are Crucial: Regular evaluations of both physical and social security measures ensure continuous improvement and adaptation to emerging threats.

By combining these strategies, condominium and high-rise communities can develop an effective, layered approach to security that not only deters crime but also nurtures a sense of belonging and trust among residents.

# CHAPTER 7

## *Security and Concierge Services*

Security and concierge services in Canadian High-Rise building such as condominiums play a pivotal role in ensuring the safety, comfort, and convenience of residents. Whether provided by a contract security provider or in-house employees, these services must comply with the *Private Security and Investigative Services Act*, which dictates the standards for training, conduct, and appearance of security personnel. This chapter explores the legislative framework, the importance of post orders, incident reporting, the scope of security personnel's duties, workplace safety, and collaboration between the condominium and security company to ensure effective service delivery.

## Legislative Framework

The provision of security services in ONTARIO residential buildings and condominiums is governed by the *Private Security and Investigative Services Act*. This Act mandates specific requirements for security guards, such as carrying a provincial security license and wearing identification tags. The Act ensures that security services are standardized and regulated, much like the *Condominium Act* governs condominium operations. Compliance with these regulations is essential for maintaining legal and effective security services. Managers in other provinces are recommended to check out the legislation that guides their security companies and ensure they are in compliance.

## What is the difference between a Concierge and Security Guard?

In the realm of condominium management, the roles of a security guard and a concierge, though occasionally overlapping, serve distinct purposes and embody different responsibilities. A condominium security guard primarily focuses on the safety and security of the building and its residents. Their duties include monitoring surveillance systems, conducting regular patrols, responding to emergencies, enforcing building rules, and ensuring that unauthorized individuals do not gain access to the premises. On the other hand, a condominium concierge provides a more personalized, customer service-oriented role. They assist residents with a variety of tasks such as receiving packages, managing guest access, coordinating with service providers, and offering information about local amenities and services. While both positions aim to enhance the living experience within the condominium, the security guard prioritizes protection and vigilance, whereas the concierge emphasizes convenience and resident satisfaction.

However, due to limiting budgets, we often see one person fulfilling both roles at most condominiums. One of the risks that we see a high rise in buildings exposed to is when buildings seek to reduce budgets by adding security duties into the concierge role. This can work if the concierge has a security license and is properly trained to add these duties to their scope of work. The risk comes from when a concierge without a security license undertakes duties such as security patrols. This could be an issue for a building if the concierge were to ever be injured during these duties.

## Practical Implementation

To ensure compliance and professionalism, property managers should:

1. Require that all personnel performing security tasks hold valid security licenses, regardless of their primary role. This includes buildings who rely on superintendents or cleaners to remove trespassers from the site.

2. Invest in ongoing training for dual-role staff to enhance their skills in both security and customer service.

3. Conduct regular audits to verify compliance with PSISA and other regulatory requirements.

By prioritizing licensing and training, condominiums can create a safer, more efficient environment for residents. Licensed security guards in dual roles provide the expertise needed to navigate complex situations, offering peace of mind to residents and ensuring that the building's management upholds the highest standards of safety and professionalism.

## How Much Security is Required?

One effective method to determine the security requirements for a building is to use a risk matrix that aligns crime trends on one axis with potential targets on the other. This approach provides an objective framework for assessing vulnerabilities and prioritizing security measures. The crime trends axis captures the frequency and severity of incidents in the surrounding area, such as thefts, vandalism, or violent crimes, while the potential targets axis identifies the number of assets (people) within the building that could attract criminal activity, including residents, vehicles, or valuable property. By plotting these factors, property managers and security professionals can visually identify high-risk areas and tailor security measures to match the specific needs of the building. For example, a condominium in a high-crime area with exposed parking structures would fall into a high-risk quadrant, warranting measures like enhanced surveillance, access controls, and full-time security. Conversely, a low-crime area with fewer potential targets might require a lighter security presence, such as mobile patrols. This matrix not only ensures that resources are allocated efficiently but also provides a defensible rationale for the level of security implemented. A copy of this matrix is included in Security Audits and Risk Reports.

## Vertical - Number of Units in a Building

1. **Potential Targets**: The number of units indicates the number of potential targets within the building. More residents mean more valuable items, such as bikes, lockers, and vehicles, which can be attractive to criminals.

2. **Security Budget**: A higher number of residents typically translates to a larger security budget, enabling more comprehensive security measures.

## Horizontal - Crime per Capita in the Building's Ward

1. **Higher Crime Rate**: Buildings located in wards with higher crime rates than the city average are at greater risk and require enhanced security measures.

2. **Crime Rate Increases**: Wards experiencing significant year-over-year increases in crime rates need to adapt their security strategies to address the escalating threat. Also, the clearance rate for the crime should be investigated.

## Security Response Levels

- In a low-risk scenario, security measures consist of random mobile patrols of the building, conducted at a frequency of 3 to 7 patrols per week.

- For minor risk, nightly patrols of the property are recommended, with patrols occurring 7 to 14 times per week.

- In medium-risk situations, a static guard is deployed during high-risk days, such as weekends, while mobile patrols cover off-risk days.

- For significant risk levels, a static guard is posted every night during high-risk hours, supported by mobile patrols during non-risk hours.

- In high-risk situations, full coverage is necessary, with a guard posted to the site 24 hours a day.

Certain multipliers may necessitate elevating a building's risk level. A high intrusion rate, defined as six or more intrusions per month, should result in a building being elevated to the next risk level. Buildings of significant size, such as those with shared facilities or commercial entrances that remain open, may also require an elevated risk level. In high-risk situations, a combination of high-risk shifts and full coverage may be needed. Lastly, buildings located in areas that attract intrusions should consider moving up a risk level to ensure adequate security measures. A breakdown of this is as below:

## Low Risk

- **Security Measures:** Random mobile patrols of the building
- **Frequency:** 3-7 patrols per week

## Minor Risk

- **Security Measures:** Nightly patrols of the property
- **Frequency:** 7-14 patrols per week

## Medium Risk

- **Security Measures:** Static Guard during high-risk days (e.g., weekends), supported by mobile patrols during off-risk days

## Significant Risk

- **Security Measures:** Static Guard posted every night during high-risk hours, with mobile patrols during non-risk hours

## High Risk

- **Security Measures:** Full Coverage - Guard posted to the site 24-hours

## Multipliers

1. **High Intrusion Rate:** If the building records six or more intrusions per month, it should be elevated to the next risk level.

2. **Significant Size:** Buildings with shared facilities or commercial entrances that remain open may require an elevated risk level. For

High Risk, combining a high-risk shift with full coverage might be necessary.

3. **Attraction Magnets**: Buildings in areas attracting intrusions should consider moving up a risk level.

Condominium and property owners / managers frequently face challenges in persuading board members and owners of the essential security requirements within their buildings. Often, the tendency is to take the easier route, neglecting the necessity for proper security measures to avoid conflict. Utilizing the 3D Security and Emergency Risk Diagram allows for an objective assessment and presentation of your building's security needs. This approach ensures that decisions are based on comprehensive risk evaluations rather than convenience.

## High Risk Hours

For condominiums and high-rise buildings that cannot afford 24-hour security coverage, scheduling security guards during high-risk hours is a practical solution to deter criminal activity and promote resident safety. High-risk hours can be determined through a combination of security audits and analysis of historical incident data. Typically, these hours are during the night when visibility is low and there are fewer residents moving around (Natural Surveillance), making it easier for potential intruders to operate unnoticed and without risk.

This book would recommend conducting thorough security audits to identify specific vulnerabilities and patterns of incidents unique to each condominium. These audits help in pinpointing the times when enhanced security presence is most needed. Additionally, incorporating Crime Prevention Through Environmental Design (CPTED) principles can further bolster safety by designing environments that naturally deter criminal activity. For those that want to take it a step further, management can use an Adversary Sequence Diagram (ASD).

Adversary Sequence Diagrams (ASDs) offer a visual tool for identifying and mitigating vulnerabilities in high-rise buildings. By plotting the steps an adversary might take to breach the existing security solutions. ASDs provide a graphic representation of potential attack vectors and weaknesses within the building's security infrastructure. This method involves mapping out each phase of a potential intrusion, from initial surveillance and planning to the final execution of the attack. By understanding these sequences, security professionals can pinpoint critical vulnerabilities, assess the effectiveness of existing security measures/response, and develop targeted strategies to bolster defenses. Implementing ASDs discussions, with security professionals, allows high-rise and condominium managers to "game out" security gaps, enhance situational awareness, and ultimately create a more resilient and secure environment for residents and occupants.

By utilizing ADS and strategically deploying security guards during these high-risk periods, building managers can ensure residents that their safety is prioritized. This approach ensures that resources are utilized effectively while maintaining a secure living environment.

## Mobile Patrol

For buildings without the resources for either 24-hour security or a guard during high-risk hours, mobile security patrols offer a flexible and effective solution. Most reputable and professional security companies will provide mobile security options that can be tailored to the specific needs of each building, ensuring comprehensive coverage without the need for on-site guards. These mobile units conduct regular patrols, check for any security breaches, and respond promptly to incidents, thereby maintaining a high level of security. This service is particularly beneficial for smaller buildings and condominiums or those with budget constraints, as it ensures safety and peace of mind for residents. As mentioned in the previous section of CPTED, ensuring residents can report concerns is important.

## Post Orders and Regular Review

Site-specific instructions, known as post or standing orders, are crucial for defining how security guards will conduct their security duties while at the property. These orders should be reviewed and approved by the Property Manager and/or the Board of Directors. Regular reviews of post orders are essential to adapt to changing security needs, emerging crime trends, and ensure alignment with current security best practices. A proactive approach by the Board and Property Manager can identify potential security gaps and update procedures, accordingly, thus maintaining a high standard of security. Part of this may include assigning a committee or advocate for building security.

In large properties, this role could be taken on by a committee. To be successful, this committee must be given a clear mandate of their responsibilities. This advocate (or committee) should be put in place to develop a high-level overview of security best practices and how they can be applied to the building. This mandate should include identifying vulnerabilities (either discovered by the committee, reported by residents, or because of a professional security review like a SA or TRA), assessing the level of risk they pose, and presenting solutions or options to either the manager and/or board of directors.

Our experience suggests this role is better fulfilled by someone other than the property manager, primarily due to the workload and the dynamic between board members and the manager. Managers are often overworked, and there is a reported shortage of managers. An effective advocate must be prepared to state and **defend** their case (and budget) at meetings, even when vastly outnumbered by those seeking to reduce costs. This advocacy process assures residents that security issues are being properly discussed and not "swept under the rug" to save on fees or because the manager is not able to argue the need for security against their client.

## Importance of Incident Reports

Incident reports are a critical component of building security management. These reports document all security-related events, providing a comprehensive record that can be reviewed and analyzed. It is imperative for buildings to keep a searchable record of these reports. Such records help in identifying trends, improving security measures, and ensuring accountability. Timely and accurate incident reporting also assists in legal and insurance matters, safeguarding the buildings' interests. It is imperative that a notification system be set up so that management receive these reports in a timely manner. The more automatic the system is, the more effective will be the results and follow-up.

## Scope of Security Personnel's Duties

Security personnel should focus solely on security-related duties and not be diverted to non-security tasks like cleaning or maintenance. Their primary responsibilities include monitoring access points, patrolling the property, and responding to emergencies. However, there is often pressured to maximize the value of security budgets by assigning guards additional non-security tasks. While this may seem cost-effective, it carries significant risks.

Assigning non-security tasks not only undermines the guard's ability to focus on their core responsibilities but also creates potential liability for the property. For instance, if a security guard is injured while performing duties outside their scope, such as mopping floors or repairing equipment, the property could face legal and financial consequences. Such incidents can result in increased insurance claims, worker's compensation disputes, and reputational damage for the property management.

Additionally, when security personnel are diverted from their primary roles, the effectiveness of security operations is compromised. If a security guard misses a critical incident—such as an unauthorized entry or an escalating conflict—because they were occupied with non-security tasks, it reflects poorly not only on the property but also on the private security industry. These failures can lead to residents and stakeholders questioning the reliability and professionalism of the security team.

To preserve the integrity of security operations and ensure residents and property are adequately safeguarded, it is essential that security staff focus exclusively on their designated roles. This specialization ensures they are always alert, responsive, and prepared to handle security concerns, reinforcing the trust and confidence placed in them by the property and its residents.

## Using Security to Supervise Moves Escort Contractors

Multi-family buildings face numerous logistical challenges, particularly when it comes to supervising moves and escorting contractors into units. Employing dedicated security services for these tasks offers several advantages that enhance overall building management and security.

The primary benefit of using security personnel for supervising moves and escorting contractors is that it significantly frees up any superintendent's time. Superintendents have a wide range of duties and skills, and as such it would not be effective to use these resources to have them monitor a move. Having a guard in place allows the superintendent to focus on the smooth operation of the building, addressing maintenance issues, and ensuring the general upkeep of the property. By delegating these tasks to security personnel, the superintendent can better manage their workload and prioritize more critical, highly skilled, operational responsibilities. During the move, security guards ensure that only authorized individuals enter the building, reducing the risk of unauthorized access and potential security breaches. This is especially important during moves or when contractors are working in the units, as these activities can create opportunities for unauthorized entry if not properly monitored.

## Escort Contractors

Using security guards to escort contractors in condominiums and high-rise buildings offers significant advantages for both residents and property management. By assigning licensed security professionals to accompany contractors, superintendents are freed from the time-consuming task of monitoring contractors, allowing them to focus on their primary responsibilities. For residents, this practice provides peace of mind, ensuring that any access to their units is supervised by a trained and trustworthy professional. This not only enhances the security of individual units but also fosters a sense of safety and trust within the building, demonstrating a proactive commitment to safeguarding residents' properties and privacy.

## Workplace Safety and Right to Refuse Unsafe Work

The safety of security personnel is paramount. Both the building management and the security company share the responsibility of providing a safe and harassment-free working environment. Security staff have the right to refuse unsafe work, and it is crucial for the management to address any safety concerns promptly. Regular safety audits and risk assessments can help identify and mitigate potential hazards, ensuring that security personnel can perform their duties without undue risk. These risk assessments should be shared with all stakeholders of the building (owners, board members, etc.).

Unfortunately, in many cases, security guards are expected to patrol alone in areas where **even** police officers would typically patrol in pairs. These isolated patrols often include stairwells, basements, and parking garages—areas that are frequently poorly lit, have limited visibility, and, critically, suffer from little or no cell phone or radio service. This lack of reliable communication dramatically increases the risk to guards, leaving them unable to call for backup or assistance during emergencies.

Such conditions have led to tragic consequences, including injuries and fatalities, as seen in 2024. This highlights not only the inherent dangers of these environments but also a systemic undervaluation of the risks faced by security personnel. It underscores the urgent need for immediate action to prioritize their safety and well-being.

Building management and security companies must reassess and improve patrol protocols to address these vulnerabilities. Solutions include ensuring that high-risk areas have robust communication infrastructure, such as signal boosters for radios and phones, implementing paired patrols in these locations, and equipping guards with personal alarm systems that function independently of standard communication networks. Additionally, frequent risk assessments and scenario-based training tailored to these environments can help guards better prepare for and respond to potential threats.

Addressing these issues is not only a matter of compliance but a critical step toward valuing the lives and contributions of security personnel, ensuring they can perform their duties with the confidence and support they deserve.

## Collaboration Between Building and Security Company

Effective collaboration between the building staff and the security company is essential for successful security operations. This partnership involves regular communication, joint training sessions, and shared objectives. Ensuring that all security staff are well-trained and understand the specific needs of the condominium enhances their ability to perform their duties effectively. Custom-designed security solutions, continuous improvement initiatives, and the use of advanced security technologies can further bolster the security framework of the condominium.

## Importance of Comprehensive Training

In the realm of condominium and high-rise security, the role of security guards and concierges extends far beyond mere presence and observation. These individuals are the first line of defense, and their actions can significantly impact on the safety and well-being of all residents and visitors. Therefore, investing in comprehensive training for security personnel is crucial. This training should go beyond site-specific protocols to include essential skills such as Use of Force, First Aid, Verbal Judo, and Emergency Management, to name a few.

## Use of Force

Training security guards in the Use of Force is critical for ensuring they can handle confrontational situations effectively and safely. Proper *Use of Force* training provides guards with the knowledge and techniques to de-escalate potentially dangerous situations and use physical force only when necessary and appropriate. This training helps in:

1. **Preventing Excessive Force:** Guards learn to assess situations accurately and apply the minimum force required, reducing the risk of injury to residents and themselves.

2. **Legal Compliance:** Proper training ensures that security personnel act within legal boundaries, protecting the condominium management from liability.

3. **Confidence and Preparedness:** Well-trained guards are more confident in their ability to handle threats, leading to a safer environment for everyone.

## First Aid

First aid training is a vital component of any comprehensive security training program. Security personnel often act as immediate responders in emergencies, and their ability to provide timely care can save lives. This need is particularly pronounced in large, high-rise buildings where paramedic response times may be extended due to logistical challenges. While horizontal travel time—getting to the building—is typically short, vertical travel time—moving within the building to the unit—can introduce delays.

Security guards trained in first aid contribute significantly to the safety of residents and staff by addressing medical emergencies effectively.

## Key benefits include:

**Immediate Response:** Trained guards can provide life-saving assistance during medical emergencies such as heart attacks, injuries, or accidents, stabilizing individuals until professional medical help arrives.

**Enhanced Safety:** Knowledge of first aid procedures fosters a safer living environment by enabling guards to address minor injuries promptly and prevent complications.

**Resident Trust:** A well-trained security team reassures residents, fostering trust and a sense of security within the community.

**Compliance with WSIB Requirements:** In Ontario, the Workplace Safety and Insurance Board (WSIB) sets out clear requirements for first aid training in workplaces, including residential buildings. These requirements ensure an immediate and effective response to medical emergencies, thereby minimizing injury severity and potentially saving lives. The WSIB mandates that:

- **Adequate First Aid Training:** At least one employee per shift must hold a valid first aid certificate.

- **Availability of First Aid Kits:** Properly stocked and accessible first aid kits must be available to all staff.

- **Record Keeping:** Employers must maintain accurate records of all first aid treatments administered.

Property managers and security companies are advised to confirm these requirements for their specific province or state to ensure compliance.

## Certification and Ongoing Training

Security companies and property managers should prioritize both initial certification and continuous education for security personnel.

**Initial Certification:** Security guards should complete emergency-level first aid courses, including training in CPR, AED usage, and basic medical emergency response, as part of their licensing requirements.

**Ongoing Education:** Although there is no current mandate for refresher courses to renew security licenses, regular re-certification is recommended to maintain skill proficiency. Property managers are encouraged to schedule these refresher courses periodically.

**Accessibility and Readiness:** For effective first aid response, security guards must have immediate access to first aid kits.

Key considerations include:

- **Strategic Placement:** First aid kits should be strategically located at security posts, common areas, and other easily accessible locations.

- **Regular Inspections:** Frequent inspections should be conducted to ensure that first aid kits are fully stocked and that supplies have not expired.

- **Record Keeping and Continuous Improvement:** Accurate and detailed record-keeping is essential for compliance and to drive improvements in emergency response:

- **Incident Logs:** Maintain detailed records of first aid incidents, including the type of emergency, actions taken, and outcomes.

- **Review and Analysis:** Regularly analyze incident logs to identify patterns, training gaps, and opportunities for enhancing emergency preparedness.

First aid training is more than a regulatory obligation; it is a critical element of a robust safety strategy in high-rises and condominiums. By investing in the training and equipping of security personnel, property managers can ensure a safer living environment, foster resident trust, and comply with WSIB requirements. Prioritizing first aid readiness not only safeguards the community but also cultivates a culture of safety and preparedness.

## Verbal Judo / Tactical Communication

Verbal Judo, or similar de-escalation communication training, equips security personnel with the skills to de-escalate conflicts through effective communication. As anyone that has lived in a multi-family building knows that tempers can flare, and often security is tasked with calming the waters. This training is vital for maintaining a peaceful and safe environment. Key aspects include:

1. **Conflict Resolution:** Guards learn techniques to calm aggressive individuals and resolve disputes without physical confrontation.

2. **Building Rapport:** Effective communication fosters better relationships between security personnel and residents, promoting a cooperative atmosphere and establishing trust. As noted in the section on 2nd generation CPTED, this trust is a critical aspect of social cohesion.

3. **Professionalism:** Verbal Judo training enhances the overall professionalism of the security team, reflecting positively on the management and the security company.

4. **Safety:** As noted in point #1, this type of training reduces physical confrontations, which in term increases guard safety and security.

## Emergency Management

Training in Emergency Management prepares security guards and concierges to respond effectively to various emergency scenarios, including fires, natural disasters, and security threats. This training involves:

1. **Preparedness:** Guards are trained to recognize potential hazards and work within proactive plans to mitigate risks.

2. **Coordination:** Effective emergency management training ensures that security personnel can coordinate with local emergency services, ensuring a swift and organized response.

3. **Evacuation Procedures:** Guards learn to lead and assist in building evacuations, ensuring the safety of all residents.

4. **Communication:** As an essential part of the training, the security team (and others) should be trained in how to activate, communicate and resolve an emergency. Getting the correct

information in a timely manner to the residents is a critical part of the EAP and staff training.

## Tabletop Exercises

Tabletop exercises (TTXs) are discussion-based sessions where team members meet in an informal setting to discuss their roles during an emergency and their responses to a particular emergency. TTXs are an essential part of emergency preparation for condominiums and high-rise buildings. They provide an opportunity for the management team, security personnel, and residents to discuss and rehearse their response to hypothetical scenarios without the need for physical deployment at the building. This is important when logistics and budgets prevent meeting in person

## Benefits of Tabletop Exercises:

1. **Identification of Gaps**: TTXs help identify gaps in the existing emergency plans and procedures. This can include issues such as training, communication breakdowns, resource allocation, and coordination challenges. For obvious reasons it is better to identify these gaps before an emergency event occurs.

2. **Enhancing Communication**: These exercises foster better communication among the various stakeholders, including management, security personnel, residents, and emergency services. Improved communication can lead to more efficient and coordinated responses during actual emergencies.

3. **Scenario Planning**: By discussing a wide range of scenarios, from natural disasters to security threats, participants can develop a comprehensive understanding of potential risks and the appropriate responses.

4. **Training and Education**: TTXs serve as an educational tool for residents and staff, helping them understand their roles and responsibilities during an emergency. This can increase the team

members' confidence in the process and ensure a more organized evacuation or response.

5. **Review and Improvement**: After each exercise, a debriefing session can be conducted to review the performance and identify areas for improvement. This continuous feedback loop helps in refining the emergency response plan.

## Conducting a Tabletop Exercise:

1. **Define Objectives**: Clearly define the objectives of the exercise. What do you want to achieve? Is it to test a new procedure, train new staff, or review the existing plan?

2. **Develop Scenarios**: Create realistic and relevant scenarios that could potentially affect the condominium or high-rise. This can include fires, floods, power outages, active attack situations, protests, or medical emergencies.

3. **Assemble Participants**: Gather all relevant participants, including management, security personnel, key staff members, and representatives from the resident community.

4. **Facilitate Discussion**: Lead the discussion by presenting the scenario and guiding participants through the response steps. Encourage open dialogue and allow participants to ask questions and provide input.

5. **Debrief**: Conduct a debriefing session to discuss what went well and what could be improved. Document the findings and update the emergency response plan accordingly.

## Full Emergency Drills

Full emergency drills involve the physical enactment of emergency scenarios. These drills are more intensive than tabletop exercises and provide a realistic environment to practice emergency response procedures.

**Benefits of Full Emergency Drills:**

1. **Realistic Practice**: Drills provide a hands-on opportunity for residents and staff to practice evacuations, use emergency equipment, and follow emergency procedures.

2. **Testing Equipment and Systems**: These drills allow for the testing of emergency equipment such as alarms, communication systems, and evacuation routes to ensure they are functional and effective.

3. **Building Muscle Memory**: Repeated practice helps participants develop muscle memory, making their responses more automatic (or at least not totally unfamiliar) during an actual emergency.

4. **Stress Testing**: Full drills test the ability of individuals and systems to perform under stress, highlighting any weaknesses that need to be addressed.

5. **Compliance and Readiness**: Regular drills ensure compliance with legal and safety regulations and demonstrate the building's commitment to the safety and preparedness of its residents.

**Conducting a Full Emergency Drill:**

1. **Plan Thoroughly**: Develop a detailed plan that outlines the objectives, scenarios, participants, and timeline for the drill. Coordinate with local emergency services if needed. As part of the preparation, make sure that responders are aware that testing is taking place.

2. **Inform Residents**: Notify residents well in advance about the drill, explaining its purpose and what they can expect. This helps to avoid unnecessary panic and ensures participation.

3. **Simulate Realism:** Create realistic scenarios that require the actual movement of people and the use of emergency equipment. This can include blocking exits, simulating smoke, or using role players to act as injured individuals. This book is **100% opposed** to any surprise drills to test readiness. There are many examples where people were hurt during surprise Active Attacker drills because they did not know it was a simulation,

4. **Monitor and Evaluate:** Assign observers to monitor the drill and evaluate the response of participants. This can include timing the evacuation, checking the functionality of equipment, and observing adherence to procedures.

5. **Hot Wash:** After the drill, conduct a thorough debriefing session to discuss the outcomes. Identify strengths and areas for improvement and document the findings to update the emergency response plan.

This chapter underscores the critical role that security and concierge services play in ensuring the safety, convenience, and overall quality of life in Canadian high-rise buildings such as condominiums. The chapter explores the legislative, practical, and operational aspects of these services, highlighting the necessity of a structured and proactive approach to security management. Whether through rigorous compliance with the Private Security and Investigative Services Act (PSISA), effective collaboration between property managers and security providers, or comprehensive training programs, these strategies are fundamental to creating a secure and welcoming environment for residents.

The chapter also emphasizes the importance of understanding the distinct roles of security guards and concierges, the need for proper licensing and training for dual-role staff, and the implementation of risk-based security measures tailored to specific building vulnerabilities. By adopting innovative tools like risk matrices and Adversary Sequence Diagrams (ASDs), condominium managers can make informed decisions and allocate resources effectively. Furthermore, the chapter advocates for prioritizing the safety and professionalism of security personnel through proper training, clear post orders, and adherence to workplace safety standards.

**Key Takeaways**

1. **Compliance with PSISA**: Ensuring all security personnel, including dual-role staff, are licensed and trained is critical for legal and effective service delivery. This compliance fosters professionalism and reduces liability.

2. **Role Clarity**: Clearly defining and maintaining the distinct responsibilities of security guards and concierges is essential. Assigning non-security tasks to guards undermines their effectiveness and increases risks.

3. **Risk-Based Security Measures**: Utilizing tools such as risk matrices and ASDs allows property managers to objectively assess vulnerabilities and implement tailored security solutions. This ensures resources are allocated efficiently based on crime trends and building-specific risks.

4. **Training and Professional Development:**

   o **Use of Force**: Guards must be trained to de-escalate situations and apply force judiciously to prevent excessive actions and ensure legal compliance.

   o **First Aid**: Comprehensive first aid training prepares guards to act as first responders, improving safety and fostering resident trust.

   o **Verbal Judo**: De-escalation techniques enhance communication and professionalism, reducing physical confrontations and promoting a positive community atmosphere.

   o **Emergency Management**: Training guards in preparedness, evacuation procedures, and communication ensures an organized response to crises.

5. **High-Risk Hours and Mobile Patrols**: For buildings unable to afford full-time security, focusing on high-risk hours and

employing mobile patrols can provide effective coverage within budget constraints.

6. **Incident Reporting and Post Orders**: Accurate incident reporting and regularly updated post orders are vital for monitoring trends, ensuring accountability, and maintaining high security standards.

7. **Collaboration and Advocacy**: Effective security operations require a strong partnership between building management and security companies. Assigning a dedicated security advocate or committee ensures security issues receive the attention and advocacy they deserve.

8. **Safety of Security Personnel**: Prioritizing the safety of guards through improved patrol protocols, reliable communication infrastructure, and scenario-based training is non-negotiable. A safeguard is a more effective and confident professional.

9. **Tabletop and Emergency Drills**: Regular tabletop exercises and full emergency drills prepare both residents and staff for emergencies, ensuring a swift and organized response while identifying and addressing procedural gaps.

By adhering to these principles and strategies, condominium managers can create safer, more resilient, and better-managed residential environments that meet the needs of all stakeholders.

# CHAPTER 8

## *Miscellaneous and Final Thoughts*

As we near the conclusion of this book, it's important to address the myriads of topics that, while they may not fit neatly into the previous chapters, are nonetheless crucial to the comprehensive understanding of security and emergency management in high-rise buildings and condominiums. These are the fine details, the nuanced practices, and the occasional "what if" scenarios that managers, boards, and security personnel often encounter but may not fully prepare for.

This chapter serves as a repository for these essential yet varied considerations. From smaller operational tips to strategic insights, we aim to provide practical guidance that complements the foundational knowledge already covered. Here, you'll find advice on navigating unique challenges, leveraging overlooked resources, and managing future technology. Additionally, we will revisit key themes from earlier chapters to reinforce their importance and demonstrate their applicability to these less conventional situations.

The goal is to leave no stone unturned in preparing condominium managers and boards for the complexities of maintaining secure, functional, and harmonious living environments. While these items might seem miscellaneous, they collectively contribute to a robust and effective security strategy, ensuring that no aspect of safety and security is overlooked.

Let's dive into the details and close with actionable insights that will empower you to handle the full spectrum of responsibilities and challenges within high-rise and condominium management.

Multi-Family Buildings offer a unique blend of personal and communal spaces, necessitating robust security measures to protect both individuals and property. The importance of maintaining a secure environment cannot be overstated, as it directly impacts the well-being of residents and the overall reputation and value of the property.

## Legal Implications and Responsibilities

In the dynamic and multifaceted environment of condominiums and high-rise buildings, ensuring the safety and security of residents is paramount. The responsibilities of managers and owners in this regard are extensive and critical. This section outlines the key duties that must be undertaken to create a secure living environment.

Amendments to the **Condominium Act** have increased the responsibilities of condo boards, including mandatory training for directors and stricter regulations to prevent activities that could harm residents or property. The **Occupiers' Liability Act** also plays a critical role, holding property owners, including condominium corporations, accountable for maintaining safe premises to prevent injuries.

## Economic Impact of Neglecting Security

Ignoring security can have dire financial consequences for high rise & condominium properties. Properties with poor security records often experience a significant drop in value. Potential buyers and investors are less likely to purchase units in a building perceived as unsafe, leading to decreased demand and lower property prices. Research indicates that properties in areas with higher crime rates or those that have experienced security breaches can suffer a reduction in value of up to 20%. In addition, 91% of condominium investors listed safety and security as one of their most important (if not the most important) considerations when looking to purchase an investment.

Moreover, the costs associated with legal battles, insurance claims, and potential fines for non-compliance with safety regulations can further strain the financial resources of a condominium corporation.

## Reputational Damage from Security Incidents

A major security incident can severely tarnish the reputation of a condominium. News of crimes or safety breaches can quickly spread, both locally and online, deterring potential buyers and renters. For example, incidents of violent crime or significant vandalism can make headlines, casting a long shadow over the property's reputation. Even after resolving the immediate security issue, the stigma can persist, leading to long-term challenges in attracting new residents and maintaining property values. In this age of social media, security and emergency events live on the internet forever.

**Best Practices for Condominium Security**

To mitigate these risks, High-rise Buildings and Condominium Corporations should adopt comprehensive security strategies, including:

1. **Regular Safety Audits**: Conducting frequent security assessments to identify and rectify vulnerabilities in the building's infrastructure.

2. **Surveillance Systems**: Installing and maintaining advanced security cameras and alarm systems to monitor common areas and deter potential criminals.

3. **Access Control**: Implementing secure access controls, such as key fob systems, to limit entry to authorized individuals.

4. **Resident Awareness Programs**: Educating residents about security protocols and encouraging them to report suspicious activities.

5. **Emergency Preparedness**: Developing and regularly updating emergency response plans to handle various security threats effectively.

**Cybersecurity in Condominiums and Residential Buildings**

In an era where technology is deeply integrated into everyday life, cybersecurity has become a critical component of residential security. Condominiums and residential buildings, often equipped with advanced smart systems and connected devices, face unique challenges in protecting sensitive information and ensuring the safety of their digital infrastructure. This section explores the importance of cybersecurity in residential settings, common vulnerabilities, and strategies for enhancing digital security.

## The Importance of Cybersecurity in Residential Settings

The adoption of smart building technology, including keyless entry systems, security cameras, and building management systems (BMS), has streamlined operations and improved convenience for residents. However, these advancements come with risks. A breach in the cybersecurity of a building can led to unauthorized access, theft of personal information, disruption of services, and even physical security risks.

Residents often store personal data in connected devices, and their Wi-Fi networks may be linked to shared building systems. This interconnectedness means that a single weak point in the building's cybersecurity can compromise the safety and privacy of all residents. Ensuring robust cybersecurity measures is not just a matter of protecting data; it is also essential for safeguarding the physical security and peace of mind of residents.

## Common Vulnerabilities in Residential Cybersecurity

Residential buildings face a range of cybersecurity threats, including:

1. **Weak Passwords and Authentication Protocols**: Many buildings still use default or easily guessable passwords for their devices and systems. Weak authentication protocols can allow attackers to gain access to critical systems.

2. **Unsecured Networks**: Public or poorly secured Wi-Fi networks can be an entry point for hackers. Cybercriminals can exploit vulnerabilities in the network to access personal devices or building systems.

3. **Outdated Software and Firmware**: Failing to update software and firmware for smart devices and building management systems can leave them susceptible to known vulnerabilities.

4. **Inadequate Segmentation**: Without proper network segmentation, a breach in one part of the network can grant attackers access to other connected systems.

5. **Lack of Awareness Among Residents**: Residents may inadvertently expose the building's cybersecurity by using unsecure devices or sharing sensitive information without considering the risks.

6. **Third-Party Vendor Risks**: External vendors who manage building systems or provide maintenance services can introduce vulnerabilities, especially if their own cybersecurity practices are inadequate.

## Strategies for Enhancing Cybersecurity

Building a robust cybersecurity framework for condominiums and residential buildings requires a multi-faceted approach. Below are key strategies to address vulnerabilities and protect against cyber threats:

1. **Conduct Regular Risk Assessments**: Regularly assess the building's cybersecurity posture to identify vulnerabilities. This includes evaluating connected devices, networks, and third-party services.

2. **Implement Strong Authentication Measures**:

   o Use complex passwords and require regular password changes.

   o Implement two-factor authentication (2FA) for critical systems and resident accounts.

3. **Secure Networks**:

   o Use encrypted Wi-Fi networks and disable public access points were unnecessary.

   o Ensure proper network segmentation to isolate critical building systems from resident networks.

4. **Update and Patch Systems**:

   o Regularly update software and firmware for all connected devices.

       o  Employ automated systems to ensure timely patch management.

5. **Educate Residents and Staff:**

       o  Conduct regular cybersecurity training sessions for residents and staff to raise awareness about common threats like phishing and malware.

       o  Provide guidance on securing personal devices and recognizing suspicious activities.

6. **Use Reliable Vendors:**

       o  Vet third-party vendors carefully to ensure they follow robust cybersecurity practices.

       o  Require vendors to adhere to cybersecurity standards through contracts and service-level agreements.

7. **Deploy Advanced Security Measures:**

       o  Use intrusion detection and prevention systems to monitor and respond to unauthorized activities.

       o  Implement endpoint security measures for all connected devices.

8. **Develop an Incident Response Plan:**

       o  Prepare a comprehensive plan to respond to cybersecurity incidents. This should include steps for containment, mitigation, and communication with affected parties.

       o  Test the plan regularly through simulated scenarios.

## The Role of Property Managers and Boards

Property managers and condominium boards play a crucial role in ensuring cybersecurity. Their responsibilities include:

- **Policy Development**: Establish clear cybersecurity policies for residents, staff, and vendors.

- **Budget Allocation**: Allocate sufficient resources for cybersecurity measures, including hiring experts and investing in advanced technologies.

- **Oversight and Governance**: Regularly review the building's cybersecurity practices and compliance with relevant regulations.

## The Future of Cybersecurity in Residential Buildings

As technology continues to evolve, so will the threats to residential cybersecurity. The emergence of the Internet of Things (IoT) and artificial intelligence (AI) presents both opportunities and challenges. While these technologies can enhance security and convenience, they also introduce new vulnerabilities. Proactive measures, ongoing education, and a culture of cybersecurity awareness will be critical for adapting to this changing landscape.

Cybersecurity is an integral part of modern residential security. By addressing common vulnerabilities and implementing best practices, condominiums and residential buildings can protect their digital infrastructure and provide a safer environment for all residents. The collaboration between property managers, residents, and cybersecurity professionals is essential for staying ahead of evolving threats.

## Internet of Things (IOT)

The Internet of Things (IoT) has revolutionized various industries, and its impact on condominium and residential security is transformative. IoT-enabled devices offer enhanced connectivity, convenience, and control, making it easier for property managers and residents to monitor and manage security. However, the integration of IoT in residential security also presents challenges, such as cybersecurity risks and the need for robust infrastructure. This section explores the benefits, challenges, and best practices for implementing IoT in condominium and residential security.

### *Understanding IoT in Residential Security*

The Internet of Things refers to a network of interconnected devices that communicate and exchange data via the internet. In the context of residential security, IoT encompasses devices such as smart locks, security cameras, motion sensors, intercom systems, and access control solutions. These devices are often integrated into a central management system, allowing property managers and residents to monitor and control security measures in real time.

### *Benefits of IoT for Condominium and Residential Security*

*Enhanced Access Control:* IoT-enabled access control systems provide a modern alternative to traditional keys and fobs. Residents can use smartphones or biometric authentication to gain access to their units and shared facilities. Property managers can grant or revoke access remotely, improving security and convenience. For instance, temporary access codes can be issued to maintenance personnel or delivery services, reducing the risk of unauthorized entry.

*Real-Time Monitoring:* IoT security cameras and motion sensors enable 24/7 monitoring of residential areas. These devices provide live feeds and instant alerts to property managers or residents when unusual activity is detected. Advanced systems equipped with artificial intelligence can differentiate between routine and suspicious behavior, minimizing false alarms.

*Improved Emergency Response:* IoT devices can enhance emergency preparedness and response in residential settings. For example, connected smoke detectors and water leak sensors can notify residents and property managers of potential hazards immediately. Integrated systems can also automate responses, such as shutting off water supply during a leak or unlocking doors during a fire evacuation.

*Data-Driven Insights:* IoT devices collect and analyze data to identify patterns and trends in security incidents. This data can help property managers assess vulnerabilities and implement targeted improvements. For example, frequent unauthorized access attempts in specific areas may indicate the need for additional security measures.

*Enhanced Communication:* IoT intercom systems allow residents to communicate with visitors and verify their identity remotely. These systems can be integrated with smartphones, enabling residents to grant or deny access even when they are not at home. This feature is particularly valuable for condominium buildings with high visitor traffic.

## Challenges of IoT in Residential Security

*Cybersecurity Risks:* The connectivity that makes IoT devices convenient also exposes them to cyber threats. Hackers can exploit vulnerabilities in poorly secured devices to gain unauthorized access or disrupt operations. A single compromised device can jeopardize the security of the entire system.

*Privacy Concerns:* IoT devices collect vast amounts of data, including video footage and access logs. Improper handling of this data can lead to privacy violations. Residents may be concerned about who has access to their data and how it is used.

*Infrastructure Requirements:* IoT systems require robust infrastructure, including high-speed internet, reliable power supply, and secure networking protocols. Older condominium buildings may face challenges in retrofitting these systems due to structural limitations or budget constraints.

*Device Interoperability:* The effectiveness of an IoT security system depends on the seamless integration of devices from different manufacturers. Lack of standardization can result in compatibility issues, complicating installation and maintenance.

*Cost Implications:* While IoT devices can provide long-term cost savings through improved efficiency, the initial investment can be significant.

Property managers and condominium boards may need to weigh the benefits against the upfront costs and ongoing maintenance expenses.

## Best Practices for Implementing IoT in Residential Security

*Prioritize Cybersecurity:* To mitigate cybersecurity risks, property managers should work with reputable vendors that prioritize device security. Implementing strong passwords, regular software updates, and encrypted data transmission can enhance system resilience. Conducting periodic security audits is also essential.

*Engage Stakeholders:* Successful implementation requires collaboration among property managers, residents, and vendors. Conducting workshops or surveys can help identify the specific needs and concerns of residents. Clear communication about the benefits and safeguards of IoT systems can foster acceptance and trust.

*Invest in Scalable Solutions:* IoT technology evolves rapidly, and property managers should choose systems that can accommodate future upgrades. Scalable solutions ensure that the security infrastructure remains relevant and effective over time.

*Address Privacy Concerns:* Establish clear policies for data collection, storage, and access. Inform residents about how their data will be used and who will have access to it. Transparency and adherence to privacy regulations can build confidence in the system.

*Conduct Training and Support:* Providing training for property managers and residents ensures that they can use IoT devices effectively. Vendors should offer ongoing support and maintenance to address technical issues promptly.

*Test and Monitor Systems:* Regular testing of IoT devices ensures that they function as intended. Monitoring system performance can help identify and address issues before they escalate. Automated diagnostics and alerts can streamline maintenance.

## Future Trends in IoT and Residential Security

As IoT technology continues to evolve, several trends are shaping its application in residential security:

*Integration with Smart Home Systems:* IoT security devices are increasingly integrated with broader smart home ecosystems, allowing residents to control lighting, climate, and entertainment alongside security features. This integration enhances convenience and creates a more cohesive user experience.

*Artificial Intelligence and Machine Learning:* AI and machine learning enable IoT devices to learn from data and improve over time. For example, security cameras can recognize familiar faces or vehicles, reducing false alarms and enhancing threat detection.

*5G Connectivity:* The rollout of 5G networks is expected to improve the reliability and responsiveness of IoT systems. Faster data transmission and lower latency will enable real-time monitoring and control on a larger scale.

*Focus on Sustainability:* IoT devices are being designed with energy efficiency in mind, reducing their environmental impact. Solar-powered cameras and energy-saving sensors are examples of sustainable innovations.

*Customizable Solutions:* Vendors are offering more customizable IoT solutions to meet the unique needs of different residential communities. Tailored systems can address specific security challenges and enhance user satisfaction.

The Internet of Things is transforming condominium and residential security by providing innovative solutions that enhance safety, convenience, and efficiency. However, the adoption of IoT also presents challenges that require careful planning and management. By prioritizing cybersecurity, engaging stakeholders, and investing in scalable and reliable systems, property managers can harness the potential of IoT to create secure and connected residential environments. As technology continues to evolve, IoT is poised to play an even greater role in shaping the future of residential security.

## Intrusion Detection Systems (IDS)

As residential communities face evolving security challenges, the integration of advanced Intrusion Detection Systems (IDS) has become a cornerstone for enhancing the safety and security of condominium and apartment buildings. These systems, equipped with cutting-edge technology, offer a proactive approach to detecting and mitigating threats before they escalate, ensuring peace of mind for residents and property managers alike. This article explores the importance of IDS, their components, benefits, and best practices for implementation in residential settings.

## What Are Intrusion Detection Systems?

Intrusion Detection Systems are designed to monitor, detect, and alert security teams or residents to unauthorized access or suspicious activities within a defined perimeter. IDS can be categorized into two primary types:

1. Perimeter Detection Systems: These systems monitor the boundaries of a property, such as fences, gates, or walls, using sensors, cameras, or other technologies.

2. Interior Detection Systems: These focus on detecting unauthorized access within a building, often using motion detectors, door/window sensors, or video surveillance.

Modern IDS often integrate with building management systems and can provide real-time alerts, video feeds, and detailed analytics to enhance decision-making during security breaches.

IDS setup typically includes:

- Sensors: Devices such as motion detectors, glass-break sensors, and infrared beams to detect physical breaches.

- Cameras: High-definition, often AI-enabled, cameras to monitor activities and provide visual evidence.

- Control Panels: The central hub that processes sensor data and triggers alarms or notifications.

- Alarms: Audible or visual alarms that alert residents and security personnel to potential threats.

- Integration with Access Control Systems: To manage and monitor entry points, ensuring only authorized individuals have access.

## Benefits of IDS in Residential Settings

1. IDS provide real-time detection of unauthorized access, enabling swift response to potential threats.

2. Visible IDS components, such as cameras and sensors, act as deterrents to potential intruders.

3. Integrated systems can automatically notify local law enforcement or security personnel, reducing response times.

4. A robust security system instills confidence among residents, enhancing their quality of life.

5. Preventing theft, vandalism, or unauthorized access can save significant costs associated with property damage or loss.

Implementing IDS in Condominium Buildings

1. Risk Assessment: Begin with a comprehensive risk assessment to identify vulnerabilities in the building's security.

2. Customized Solutions: Tailor IDS components to the specific needs of the property, considering factors like size, layout, and crime trends in the area.

3. Integration: Ensure seamless integration with existing security infrastructure, such as access control systems and surveillance cameras.

4. Training: Educate residents and staff on the system's functionalities, emphasizing the importance of reporting suspicious activities.

5. Regular Maintenance: Schedule routine checks to ensure the system operates efficiently, addressing issues like sensor calibration or software updates.

**Challenges and Considerations**

While IDS offer numerous benefits, their implementation in residential settings is not without challenges:

- Privacy Concerns: Balancing security with residents' privacy is critical. Transparency about the purpose and scope of surveillance can help mitigate concerns.

- Cost: The initial investment can be significant, but long-term benefits often justify the expenditure.

- False Alarms: Regular maintenance and calibration are essential to minimize false alarms, which can undermine the system's credibility.

**The Future of IDS in Residential Security**

Advancements in technology are paving the way for more sophisticated IDS solutions. AI and machine learning are enabling predictive analytics, allowing systems to anticipate threats based on patterns and behaviors. Additionally, the integration of IoT devices is creating smarter, more interconnected security ecosystems.

For condominium and property managers, staying ahead of these technological trends is essential to ensuring the safety and satisfaction of residents. By investing in IDS, residential communities can foster an environment where security is not just a feature but a fundamental cornerstone of living.

Intrusion Detection Systems are rapidly becoming and integral part of modern residential security. Their ability to detect, deter, and respond to potential threats makes them invaluable in safeguarding condominium and apartment buildings. By prioritizing risk assessments, tailoring solutions, and embracing technological advancements, property managers can create a secure living environment that meets the needs of today's residents.

For property managers considering IDS implementation, the key is to focus on systems that provide robust protection while aligning with the community's unique needs. A well-designed IDS not only protects property but also builds trust and confidence among residents, reinforcing the value of proactive security measures.

## HUMAN RISK - Dealing with Problem Residents

### Step 1: Document Everything

The first step in addressing problem residents is to document all incidents meticulously. Proper documentation ensures that there is a clear record of the unacceptable behavior, which is crucial for any future actions that may need to be taken. Here are some key practices:

- **Incident Reports:** Security personnel and management should maintain detailed incident reports. These should include dates, times, descriptions of the behavior, and any witnesses.

- **Resident Reporting Mechanism:** Establish a reliable and easy-to-use mechanism for residents to report concerns. This could be an online portal, a dedicated phone line, or a specific email address.

- **Security Awareness:** Make security teams aware of the situation from the onset. They should monitor the situation closely and document any further incidents.

## Step 2: Escalation to Authorities

If the problematic behavior persists, it becomes necessary to involve higher authorities. This involves notifying the police and consulting with the condominium's legal team. The problem residents should be formally warned about the potential consequences of their continued behavior.

- **Police Involvement**: If the situation poses a threat to the safety of other residents or property, contacting the police is essential. Ensure that all documented evidence is ready to be presented.

- **Legal Consultation**: Engage the condominium's lawyer to understand the legal options available. This might include issuing formal warnings or starting emergency eviction proceedings. It is essential to start this process before any incidents start to escalate in severity and frequency.

- **Formal Warnings**: Issue a formal warning to the resident, stating that continued unacceptable behavior will result in escalated measures and associated costs.

## Step 3: Implementing the "Reverse Bodyguard" or "Behavior Escort"

In extreme cases, where the behavior continues to deteriorate, implementing more drastic measures may be necessary. This includes what 3D Security and Emergency Response Services call "The Reverse Bodyguard" or the "Behavior Escort".

- **Assignment of Security Personnel**: A security guard is assigned to accompany the problem residents whenever they are in the common areas. This ensures the safety of other residents and the property.

- **Specialized Training for Guards**: Security personnel need specialized training to handle the higher risk involved in such situations. This includes conflict resolution, de-escalation techniques, and constant vigilance.

- **Access Control**: In consultation with the building's legal team, it is recommended that access control be limited to a certain number of doors to allow the security team to be able to monitor the residents.

- **Cost Implications**: Inform the problem resident that the costs incurred for these additional security measures may be sought from them. This serves as a deterrent and emphasizes the seriousness of their behavior. At the time of writing, recent law cases have found the residents to be held responsible for the financial burdens that extra security efforts cost the building.

## Human Risk - Dealing with Trespassers

Trespassers are one of the most common intrusions faced by condominiums and residential buildings. These incidents range from harmless loitering to more serious unauthorized entries that can threaten the safety and security of residents. Addressing trespassing effectively requires a combination of proactive measures, clear protocols, and appropriate responses tailored to the building's resources and circumstances. This section provides strategies for managing trespassers, whether your building has an on-site security team or relies on alternative measures.

### For Buildings with an On-Site Security Team:

1. **Establish Clear Protocols:** Security teams should have predefined protocols for identifying, confronting, and managing trespassers. This includes steps for escalation if a trespasser becomes uncooperative.

2. **Use of Surveillance Tools:** Leverage security cameras and access control systems to monitor and document trespassing incidents. This ensures evidence is available for legal action if needed.

3. **Communication and Coordination:** Ensure security staff are equipped with reliable communication devices. Immediate

reporting and coordination among team members are essential for effectively managing trespassers.

4. **Engagement Techniques:** Train security personnel in de-escalation tactics and verbal judo to resolve situations without conflict wherever possible.

5. **Regular Training:** Conduct scenario-based training sessions for the security team to prepare for various trespassing scenarios, from passive loiterers to potentially aggressive individuals.

**For Buildings Without an On-Site Security Team:**

1. **Community Awareness:** Educate residents or tenants on recognizing and reporting trespassers. Encourage the use of designated reporting channels, such as a property manager or a security hotline.

2. **Enhance Physical Security:** Install measures like key fob access systems, surveillance cameras, and motion-activated lighting to deter unauthorized access.

3. **Establish a Response Plan:** Create a clear plan for dealing with trespassers. Include details on who to contact (e.g., property management, local law enforcement) and steps to ensure personal safety while addressing the situation.

4. **Leverage Technology:** Consider implementing remote monitoring services where security professionals can intervene via intercom systems or dispatch local law enforcement if necessary.

5. **Signage and Deterrence:** Post clear signs around the property stating that trespassing is prohibited and under surveillance. Visual deterrents can often prevent potential incidents.

**General Considerations:**

**Legal Compliance**

All actions taken against trespassers must align with local laws to ensure compliance and to avoid potential liability. It is critical to understand and adhere to the applicable legal framework when addressing trespassing incidents.

**Documentation**

Incidents involving trespassers should be thoroughly documented. This includes recording the date, time, a detailed description of the individuals involved, and a comprehensive account of the actions taken. Proper documentation is essential for maintaining accurate records and supporting any subsequent legal or procedural actions.

**Safety First**

The safety of residents, staff, and all individuals involved must be the top priority when managing trespassing incidents. Measures should be implemented to minimize risks and ensure that responses to trespassing situations are handled in a manner that prioritizes well-being and reduces potential harm.

**Thank you:**

As we conclude this journey through the essential aspects of residential security, I want to take a moment to sincerely thank you, our valued reader, for investing your time and energy into understanding the complexities and best practices of keeping our homes and communities safe. Your decision to educate yourself on these critical matters is a testament to your dedication to creating a secure environment for yourself, your loved ones, and your neighbors.

This book was crafted with the hope that it would serve as a comprehensive guide, equipping you with the tools and insights necessary to navigate the evolving challenges of residential security. From understanding the nuances of access control and emergency preparedness to addressing the human factors that influence security outcomes, we have covered a broad spectrum of topics designed to empower you in your role—whether as a resident, property manager, or security professional.

Remember, security is not a static concept. It requires continuous learning, adaptation, and collaboration. As you implement the strategies and principles outlined in these pages, I encourage you to remain vigilant, proactive, and open to new ideas.

If you have any questions, need further clarification, or believe that my team and I at 3D Security and Emergency Response Services can assist you in enhancing your building's security, please don't hesitate to reach out.

A QR code is provided below for your convenience, offering direct access to our resources and contact information.

Thank you again for allowing me to share my expertise and passion for residential security with you. I hope this book becomes a valuable resource on your journey toward building a safer community.

Yours in Safety and Respect,

*Scott Hill*
Scott Hill, RCM, PSP, CPP

Book Here

# APPENDIX

## *Security Checklist*

3D Security Service
Security Checklist

Number________________________ Date: ____________

Address: ______________________________________________

______________________________________________

______________________________________________

**Perimeter Protection:**

| Direction | Boundary (street) | Protection (fence, hedge) | Comments |
|---|---|---|---|
| North | | | |
| South | | | |
| East | | | |
| West | | | |

Signage: ______________________________________________

______________________________________________

______________________________________________

3D Security Service
Security Checklist

## <u>ACCESS CONTROL</u>

Entry System - _____

Manual or user website on site: _____

Controlled Location: _____

On back-up power _____

Back-up/ surge protection: _____

Lockboxes (condo) _____

Lockboxes (real estate) _____

Master Key Location _____

Layered Security _____

Presence of Prop Alarms: _____

Possible to access Building through utility services: _____

Is there a loading dock for condo moves? _____

Are ground floor windows vulnerable? _____

Common element door frame construction _____

Unit door frame construction _____

Unit lock type _____

Are non-window openings protected? _____

Are elevators integrated into fob system? _____

Restricted gatway keys in use / high security keys: _____

3D Security Service
Security Checklist

Listing of Doors / Protection:

| Door | Protected | Door | Protected |
|------|-----------|------|-----------|
|      |           |      |           |
|      |           |      |           |
|      |           |      |           |
|      |           |      |           |
|      |           |      |           |
|      |           |      |           |
|      |           |      |           |
|      |           |      |           |
|      |           |      |           |

*Notes:*

3D Security Service
Security Checklist

## Video Surveillance System

\# of cameras in system: _____

Possible to enter building without being caught on camera?

Archived footage: _____

Backed-up: _____

Room for expansion: _____

Expansion needed? _____

Who has access? _____

On emergency power? _____

Transmission Media (fibre, network, coaxial, telephone): _____

Monitored real time or recorded: _____

### Notes:

3D Security Service
Security Checklist

| Location | Rating | Priority |
|----------|--------|----------|
|  |  |  |
|  |  |  |
|  |  |  |
|  |  |  |
|  |  |  |
|  |  |  |
|  |  |  |
|  |  |  |
|  |  |  |
|  |  |  |
|  |  |  |
|  |  |  |
|  |  |  |
|  |  |  |
|  |  |  |
|  |  |  |
|  |  |  |
|  |  |  |
|  |  |  |
|  |  |  |
|  |  |  |
|  |  |  |
|  |  |  |
|  |  |  |
|  |  |  |

*On back of Sheet:  Recommended location of expansion cameras*

*Appendix*

3D Security Service
Security Checklist

**3D SECURITY SERVICES**

## Lighting:

Lighting at main entrances: _____

Lighting pointing at boundaries: _____

Any occupancy lighting? _____

Is stairwell and exit sign lighting operational: _____

| Location | Reading | Location | Reading |
|----------|---------|----------|---------|
|          |         |          |         |
|          |         |          |         |
|          |         |          |         |
|          |         |          |         |
|          |         |          |         |
|          |         |          |         |
|          |         |          |         |
|          |         |          |         |
|          |         |          |         |
|          |         |          |         |
|          |         |          |         |
|          |         |          |         |
|          |         |          |         |
|          |         |          |         |
|          |         |          |         |
|          |         |          |         |

*On Back of Sheet: Recommended locations for extra lighting*

3D Security Service
Security Checklist

## Site Security

Post Orders Received & Reviewed

Do the post orders clearly define emergency procedures / responses?

What are anticipated response time to emergencies

Sample of Shift Reports received and reviewed

Incident Reports received and reviewed

Scheduled hours adequate for protection of property?

---

### *Site Inspection #1:*

Guard name: _____

Proper Uniform: _____

Security Licence: _____

Rating: _____

### *Site Inspection #2:*

Guard name: _____

Property Uniform: _____

Security Licence: _____

Rating: _____

3D Security Service
Security Checklist

*Site Inspection #3:*

Guard name: _____

Property Uniform: _____

Security Licence: _____

Rating: _____

*Site Inspection #4:*

Guard name: _____

Property Uniform: _____

Security Licence: _____

Rating: _____

***Notes:***

8 | P a g e

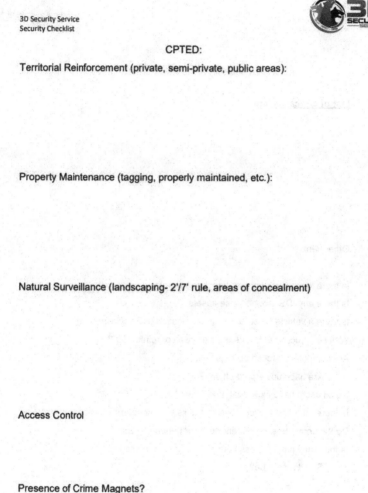

3D Security Service
Security Checklist

## CPTED:

Territorial Reinforcement (private, semi-private, public areas):

Property Maintenance (tagging, properly maintained, etc.):

Natural Surveillance (landscaping- 2'/7' rule, areas of concealment)

Access Control

Presence of Crime Magnets?

*Appendix*

**Other Security Measures:**

**List of critical assets**

Other Items:

Is there layered security around these assets:

Is there any IDS around these assets:

Is there a vehicle for security communication (RE social media):

Wall construction Critical Assets (drywall or reinforced)? _____

Are computers backed up regularly

    Are back-ups stored off site?

Do all users have individual passwords?

Is there surge protection / battery packs on computers?

Do the computers log out after a short period of inactivity

Is there any panic/duress buttons or sensors on site?

    Should there be?

Are there safes in building?

    Who has access?

    was last time combination was changed?

    Security Budget

        Are there funds in operational budget?

        Is there funds called for in the Reserve Fund Study

**Notes:**

# APPENDIX

## *Lighting Levels*

**SECURITY LIGHTING**
(Minimum Standard)

**Perimeter Fence**   2 fc.

**Site Landscape**
Walkways   1 – 4 fc.
Roadways   0.5 – 2 fc.
Entrances   10 fc.
Open Yards   2 fc.

**Building Façade**   0.5 – 2 fc.

**Indoor Parking**   5 fc.
(4 : 1 Ratio)

**Open Parking**
Low Activity   0.2 fc.
High Activity   2.0 fc.
Access Control   5.0 fc.

**Cameras**
For Detection   0.5 fc.
For Recognition   1.0 fc.
For Identification   2.0 fc.

# APPENDIX

# *Risk Rating*

## Risk Rating of Findings

| Consequence of Risk | | 6 | 5 | 4 | 3 | 2 | 1 |
|---|---|---|---|---|---|---|---|
| A: Fatal | A | | | | | | |
| B: Very Serious | B | | | | | | |
| C: Moderately Serious | C | | | | | | |
| D: Serious | D | | | | | | |
| E: Relatively unimportant | E | | | | | | |

| Probability of Risk | Almost Impossible | Highly unlikely | Unlikely but possible | Possible but unusual | Quite possible and likely | Almost Certain to occur |
|---|---|---|---|---|---|---|

|  | | Unmitigated Risk | Mitigated Risk |
|---|---|---|---|
|  | Extreme Risk | Emergency | Unacceptable Risk – take additional mitigating action |
|  | High Risk | Urgent | Unacceptable Risk – take additional mitigating action |
|  | Moderate Risk | Mitigation must be justified | Execute mitigation |
|  | Low Risk | Mitigation should not be done | Mitigation may not be justified |

# APPENDIX

# *Signage (Private Property)*

# APPENDIX

## *Signage (Reduce Tailgating)*

Printed in the United States
by Baker & Taylor Publisher Services

Printed in the United States
by Baker & Taylor Publisher Services